CHESS
FOR
JUNIORS

▚▚▚▚▚▚▚▚▚▚▚▚▚

CHESS
FOR
JUNIORS

A COMPLETE GUIDE FOR
THE BEGINNER

Robert M. Snyder

National Chess Master
and Director of Chess for Juniors

DAVID McKAY
COMPANY, INC.

Library of Congress Cataloging-in-Publication Data

Snyder, Robert M.
    Chess for juniors: a complete guide for the beginner / by Robert
M. Snyder.
       p.   cm.
   Includes index.
   Summary: Introduces the pieces, rules, opening moves, and basic
strategy of chess.
   ISBN 0-8129-1867-3
   1. Chess—Juvenile literature. [1. Chess.] I. Title.
GV1446.S59   1991
795.1'2—dc20   90-40124

Book design by M 'N O Production Services, Inc.

Chess diagrams by M-Mate-Chess

Chess drawings on pages 9, 16, 21, 23, 25, 27 by Max Perea

Manufactured in the United States of America

9 8 7 6 5

To my many students

Thanks are due to Chess for Juniors assistant coach and tournament director Calvin Olson, to my father, Alan Snyder, and to Gerald Blem, for their assistance in proofreading and reviewing the manuscript.

CONTENTS

■ CONTENTS ■

LESSON 18

DAMIANO'S DEFENSE GAME

LESSON 19

PAUL MORPHY VERSUS COUNT ISOUARD
AND THE DUKE OF BRUNSWICK

LESSON 20

CONTINUING TO IMPROVE

INTRODUCTION

You are about to learn how to play one of the world's oldest and most popular games—chess! Each player commands his own army of Knights, Bishops, Pawns, Rooks, Queens, and Kings, which battle one another on a battlefield known as a chessboard. The final objective is to attack the enemy king so that it can't escape. This is called "checkmate," and when you do this you win the game. A lot of planning and strategy go into winning, and make chess a challenging and exciting game.

Chess is a game for all ages. In the Soviet Union children learn to play chess at school. Chess teaches you important skills like logic, concentration, and abstract thinking. It may even improve school grades!

In this book I have tried to make chess as easy as possible to learn. The lessons are based on teaching methods used to introduce thousands of students to chess. After you have completed the first five lessons you will be ready to play your first game.

Begin with Lesson One and work through each of the lessons in the order that they are given. Go back and repeat any part of a lesson that you don't understand. It's important to understand the basic rules in the first four lessons and the notation in Lesson Five before you go on to Lesson Six.

You don't need a chess set for the first five lessons, but it might be good to practice each mini-lesson with a chess set. I recommend that you use a Staunton-design chess set as you proceed with the lessons in the rest of the book.

Staunton chess sets are the most common kind. They are used in tournaments and chess clubs. You'll find drawings of Staunton design pieces in Lesson Two.

Let's begin!

CHESS
FOR
JUNIORS

BACKGROUND

People have been playing chess for hundreds of years. It was played by ancient kings and knights even before the Middle Ages. When it first appeared the rules were different. However, the game has had only minor changes over the last five hundred years. When Columbus sailed in search of a shortcut to the Orient, people played chess much as they do today!

No one knows exactly how old chess is or where it was invented. One legend says that an ancient king of India wanted a game of great skill in which the players commanded a war between armies, and offered a reward to anyone who could create such a game.

A wise man created the game of chess and presented it to the king. The king loved it. At first the wise man refused the king's reward, saying that just pleasing his king was enough, but the king insisted that the wise man accept a reward.

The wise man asked that one grain of rice be given to him for the first square on the chessboard, two grains for the second square, four grains for the third square, and that on each of the following squares the number of grains

3

be double that of the last square. It didn't sound like much at first, but it adds up: it's over a *million* grains of rice for the twentieth square, and over *two million* for the next one. *And there are sixty-four squares!* By the time the thirtieth square was reached all the rice of India was used up! The wise man knew that the entire world could not supply enough rice to fill his demand.

SOME BASIC RULES

Chess is a game of pure skill. You can't win on luck alone. You'll win the game by using your army of pieces to attack the enemy King so that it has no escape. That point is called "checkmate." Checkmate is the final objective and wins the game.

Chess is played on a battlefield known as a "chessboard," which looks like this:

The Chessboard.

A chessboard has sixty-four squares which are alternately white and black. In chess, light pieces and squares are always called white, and dark pieces and squares are called black, even if the chess set has different-colored squares and pieces.

When you set up your chessboard, a white square should be positioned in the lower right-hand corner. This is easy to remember because of the rhyme "White goes on the right."

The left-to-right (horizontal) rows of squares are called ranks. The up-and-down (vertical) rows of squares are called files. The slanted (diagonal) rows of squares (all the same color) are called diagonals.

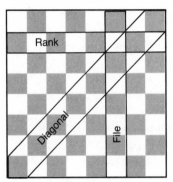

A Rank, a File, and a Diagonal.

Players take turns moving the pieces on the board, but White always makes the very first move. Each side starts out with sixteen pieces, divided up into six different types. Each type of piece moves in a particular way. Together, all the pieces are called "material." You'll find this word used later in the book.

The names of the different pieces are shown below with the symbol that is used for that piece:

♙ White Pawn	♟ Black Pawn
White Knight ♘	Black Knight ♞
♗ White Bishop	♝ Black Bishop
White Rook ♖	Black Rook ♜
♕ White Queen	♛ Black Queen
White King ♔	Black King ♚

5

Each side starts out with eight Pawns, two Knights, two Bishops, two Rooks, one Queen, and one King.

Any piece can capture an enemy piece by moving to the square occupied by the piece it is capturing. The only exception is the "en passant" capture which I'll explain later. You can only capture one enemy piece with any move.

In a game you will try to exchange your weaker, less valuable pieces for stronger enemy pieces. Each piece has a point value. Remembering the point values will help you to decide which piece you are willing to give up to capture an enemy piece. As the game progresses, the value of a piece may change. But I'll explain this later on. So just hold on and enjoy the ride!

THE STARTING POSITIONS OF THE PIECES

In Diagram 1 we have the starting positions of all the pieces.

Diagram 1. The starting positions of the pieces.

Many beginners make the mistake of setting up their Queen and King on the wrong squares, but there's an easy rule to remember: the Queen goes on the square of its own color. The White Queen goes on a white square next to the

6

King and the Black Queen goes on a black square next to the King. See Diagram 2.

Diagram 2. *The Queen starts on a square of its own color.*

2

▗▝▗▝▗▝▗▝▗▝▗▝▗▝▗▝▗▝

THE INDIVIDUAL PIECES
AND HOW THEY MOVE

(1)   ## THE PAWN

The Pawn is the foot soldier of your army. It moves slowly compared to the rest of your army. At the beginning of the game the Pawn is the weakest and least valued of the pieces. Later in the game, however, a Pawn can become very valuable.

Do not call a Pawn a Pond. There is no letter "d" at the end of this word! Keep in mind that a Paw*n* is a chess piece and a Pon*d* is a place where frogs and fish live!

The Pawn has a value of one point. It takes at least three Pawns to equal the value of the next most powerful piece.

Pawns can only move forward. In fact, the Pawn is the only chess piece that cannot move backward! On its first move each Pawn can move either one or two squares straight forward. In Diagram 3 the White Pawn hasn't been moved yet. It has the choice of moving one or two squares forward.

Diagram 3. First move: The Pawn can move to either square marked "X."

After its first move, a Pawn can move only one square forward for each move. In Diagram 4 the White Pawn has already made its first move. From now on it can only move one square forward.

The Pawn

9

Diagram 4. The Pawn can move to the square marked "X."

If the square directly in front of your Pawn is occupied, then your pawn is blocked and cannot move forward. In Diagram 5 both the White Pawn and the Black Pawn are blocked and can't move.

Diagram 5. Both Pawns are blocked and can't move.

In Diagram 6 both the White and Black Pawns can only move one square forward. The White Pawn is still in the starting position, but cannot move two squares forward because the Black Pawn blocks it.

Diagram 6. Either Pawn can move to the square marked "X."

When a Pawn captures, it uses a special move. Pawns capture by moving diagonally one square forward. In Diagram 7 the White Pawn can capture either one of the Black pieces.

Diagram 7. The White Pawn can capture either one of the Black pieces.

If the White Pawn in Diagram 7 decided to capture a Black Pawn, the position in Diagram 8 would be reached.

Diagram 8. Position after White has captured the Black Pawn.

On its first move a Pawn *cannot* capture by moving two squares diagonally. If a Pawn moves two squares forward on its first move it can't capture on that move.

THE "EN PASSANT" PAWN CAPTURE RULE

There is a very special way for a Pawn to capture, called "en passant." It's a little more complicated. "En passant" is a French term meaning "in passing." It only applies to two enemy Pawns under certain conditions.

Here's how it works. If a Pawn moves two squares forward and lands *directly beside* an enemy Pawn (on the

Diagram 9. Black's turn to move.

same rank), then the Pawn that just moved can be captured as if it had moved one square forward. If you are confused, don't worry, I'll explain the rule further.

In Diagram 9 it is Black's turn to move.

From the position in Diagram 9, the Black Pawn moves two squares forward, landing directly beside the White Pawn. That is the position in Diagram 10.

Diagram 10. *Position after the Black Pawn has moved two squares forward.*

White may now capture Black's Pawn just as if the Black Pawn had only moved one square forward. If White decides to make the capture, then the White Pawn moves diagonally behind the Black Pawn in the direction of the arrow in Diagram 10. White removes the Black Pawn from the board, reaching the position in Diagram 11.

If White didn't make the en passant capture on the first opportunity, White's pawn would lose the right to capture Black's pawn en passant. An en passant capture can only be made on the move immediately following the enemy Pawn's move. En passant can be used whenever this situation arises.

En passant is one of the least known and least understood rules of chess. Many people play chess for years

13

Diagram 11. Position after the en passant capture is made.

without knowing it. But don't worry if you do not fully understand en passant. You can come back to this section later.

PAWN PROMOTION

Do you know what happens to a Pawn when it reaches the other side of the board? I have heard many answers: "It dies," or "It turns around and comes back the other way!" Those are good tries, but they're not correct.

When a Pawn reaches the last rank (the end of the board), it can turn into any piece except a King. This is called "promotion," and *only* a Pawn can do this. When your Pawn reaches the other side of the board, you decide whether to turn it into a Knight, Bishop, Rook, or Queen. You can't promote a Pawn into an enemy piece!

In Diagram 12, when the Pawn moves one square to the last rank, it gets promoted.

When a Pawn reaches the last rank the player usually promotes it to the most powerful of all pieces, the Queen. This is called "Queening" a Pawn. You can have as many new Queens as you can get Pawns to the other side of the board. You could have as many as *nine* Queens on the board, but

14

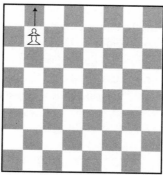

Diagram 12. The Pawn is about to be "promoted."

it's very difficult to Queen a Pawn early in the game, because there are so many enemy pieces on the board.

In Diagram 13, the White Pawn from Diagram 12 has just advanced to the last rank. White has chosen to Queen his Pawn.

Diagram 13. White has promoted the Pawn to a Queen.

Chess sets come with only one Queen for each side. If you promote a Pawn into a second Queen, you may need to borrow a Queen from another set. If another set is not available then you can turn a Rook upside down as a second Queen. (This works with most Staunton chess sets.) If a Rook is not available and you are playing a non-tournament game, put two Pawns on the same square in place of the second Queen. These are different ways of showing that your Pawn has been promoted to a Queen.

In a few rare cases it would be a good idea to promote a Pawn to a Knight, Bishop, or Rook instead of a Queen. If a Pawn is promoted to one of these pieces it is called "underpromotion."

(3) THE KNIGHT

The Knight looks like a horse. It has a value of three points, about the same as three Pawns.

It has a very tricky way of moving. A Knight can jump over its own pieces or enemy pieces. In fact, the Knight is the only piece allowed to jump over another piece.

The Knight moves in the shape of the letter "L," as shown in Diagram 14. The arrows point to the squares that the Knight can move to.

The Knight

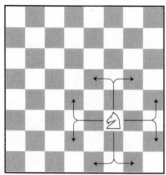

Diagram 14. *The Knight moves in an L-shape to the squares shown by arrows.*

You'll learn the movement of a Knight by remembering that it moves in two steps. It moves two squares in any straight line on a rank or file, then it *turns* and moves to another square at a right angle.

Let's look at some examples of a Knight's movement. If it moves up or down the board (vertically) on a file it would first move two squares up or down and then one square to the left or right. See Diagram 15.

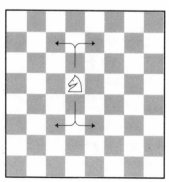

Diagram 15. *Moving a Knight up or down the board.*

If you choose to move your Knight sideways (horizontally) on a rank it would first move two squares to the left or right and then move one square up or down. See Diagram 16.

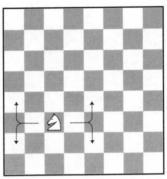

Diagram 16. Moving a Knight to the left or right.

One thing to keep in mind about the way the Knight moves: if a Knight moves from a white square it will land on a black square; or if it moves from a black square it will land on a white square. You might say, "Whenever a Knight makes a move, that's a horse of a different color!"

Diagram 17. The White Knight can capture the Black Queen.

A Knight doesn't capture any piece that it jumps over. It can capture *only* the piece occupying the square it lands on. In Diagram 17 the Knight can move to a square marked "X" or capture the Black Queen.

The position in Diagram 18 is reached after the White Knight has captured the Black Queen.

Diagram 18. *Position after the White Knight has captured the Black Queen.*

In Diagram 19 the White Knight has a choice of capturing either of the Black Pawns.

Diagram 19. *The White Knight can capture either of the Black Pawns.*

How many moves do you think it will take you to move a Knight from the lower right-hand corner of the board to the upper left-hand corner of the board? Let's try an exercise with a Knight. From Diagram 20 move the Knight from the lower right-hand corner to the square marked "X." Count how many moves it takes you.

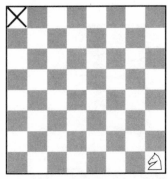

Diagram 20. *Count how many moves it takes you to move the White Knight to the square marked "X."*

If your Knight reached its goal in six moves, you did it in the shortest possible time. An example of six moves is shown in Diagram 21.

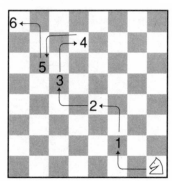

Diagram 21. *It takes six moves to move the Knight to the opposite corner.*

You are *never* allowed to capture one of your own pieces. It may sound silly, but in one game a student captured his own Queen with his Knight! His opponent began to snicker. He certainly wasn't about to tell the other student that he had captured *his own* Queen—he wanted to keep the Queen off the board. However, it wasn't long before the student who captured his own Queen noticed that it was missing! They had to start the game all over again.

If you ever notice an illegal move being made (a move that isn't allowed), you should immediately tell your opponent. Don't just snicker about it! Chess is a game of skill, and it's fun to win—but it's much more fun if you know the game was played fair and square.

THE BISHOP (3)

The Bishop is shaped like the hat that a bishop wears. Such a hat is called a miter (pronounced like "my turn" without the "n").

The Bishop is valued at three points. It is worth about the same as a Knight or three Pawns.

The Bishop

Diagram 22. The Bishop moves along the slanted rows of squares marked "X."

The Bishop moves along the slanted rows of squares of its own color, known as "diagonals." In fact, a Bishop spends the whole game on the same color square that it begins on. You begin the game with one white-squared Bishop and one black-squared Bishop. For example, the black-squared Bishop can move to any of the squares marked "X" in Diagram 22.

A Bishop can travel diagonally as far as its path is clear. It can capture the first enemy piece it runs into. In Diagram 23 the White Bishop can capture the Black Knight or move to any square marked "X."

Diagram 23. The White Bishop can capture the Black Knight.

After the White Bishop has captured the Black Knight the position in Diagram 24 is reached.

Diagram 24. *Position after the White Bishop has captured the Black Knight.*

THE ROOK ⟨5⟩

The Rook looks like a castle, but don't call it that. (There's a special move called "castling"; I'll explain it later.) Each side starts out with two Rooks, one in each corner of the board.

The Rook

The Rook has a value of five points. It is worth about the same as five Pawns or a Knight and two Pawns.

The Rook moves in straight lines, either along the ranks horizontally (left and right), or along the files vertically (up and down). It can move to any square marked "X" in Diagram 25.

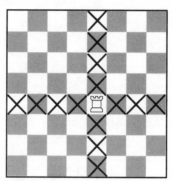

Diagram 25. The Rook can move in straight lines along the ranks and files to any square marked "X."

The Rook can travel horizontally or vertically as far as its path is clear. It can capture the first enemy piece it runs into. In Diagram 26 the Rook can capture the Black Bishop or move to any square marked "X."

Diagram 26. The White Rook can capture the Black Bishop.

After the White Rook has captured the Black Bishop the position in Diagram 27 is reached.

Diagram 27. Position after the Rook has captured the Black Bishop.

THE QUEEN (9)

The Queen is the most powerful piece. It has the combined powers of a Rook *and* a Bishop.

The Queen

25

It can move like a Rook in straight lines, both horizontally and vertically along the ranks and files. It can *also* move like a Bishop, diagonally along the slanted rows of squares of one color. In Diagram 28 it can move to any square marked "X."

The Queen has a value of nine points. It is worth about the same as a Rook and four Pawns, or a Rook, a Knight, and a Pawn.

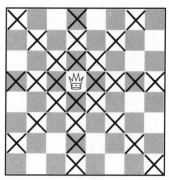

Diagram 28. *The Queen can move to any square marked "X."*

Like the Rook and the Bishop, the Queen can move along a rank, a file, or a diagonal as far as its path is clear.

Diagram 29. *The White Queen can capture the Black Rook, Pawn, or Knight—but* not *the Bishop.*

In Diagram 29 the White Queen can capture the Black Rook, Pawn, or Knight—or it can move to any square marked "X." But it cannot capture the Black Bishop.

THE KING

The King is the most important of all of the pieces. On a Staunton chess set it is the tallest of the pieces. You can recognize it as the piece with the cross on top. The cross isn't meant to keep vampires away, but you can keep a Staunton chess set in your room just in case!

The King doesn't have a point value because if the King is lost, the game is lost.

But the King is *not* a powerful piece. It can only move one square in any direction. In Diagram 30 the King can move to any square marked "X."

The King

27

Diagram 30. The King can move one square in any direction to the squares marked "X."

The King can move one square diagonally, one square on a rank (horizontally), *or* one square on a file (vertically). The King can capture an enemy piece on a square next to it. In Diagram 31 the King can capture either of the Black Pawns or move to a square marked "X."

Diagram 31. The King can capture either of the Black Pawns or move to any square marked "X."

Now you know all the pieces and how they can move—you're off to a good start!

CHECK

A piece is "attacked" when it is about to be captured by an enemy piece. When the King is placed under attack it is "in check."

Whenever an enemy piece places your King in check, you *must* always make a move to get it out of check.

You can never make a move that would leave your King in check! In Diagram 32 the Black Bishop has the White King in check.

Diagram 32. The Black Bishop has the White King in check.

29

There are three possible ways to get your King out of check:

1. Capture the enemy piece that is attacking the King.
2. Block the piece that is attacking the King. This is done by placing a piece between the King and the attacking enemy piece.
3. Move the King to a square that is not under attack by an enemy piece.

In Diagram 33 <u>any</u> of the <u>three</u> ways may be used to get

Diagram 33. *White can use three different ways to get out of check.*

Diagram 34. *The White Bishop captured the Black Rook to get the White King out of check.*

the White King out of check by the Black Rook. See if you can find them.

In Diagrams 34, 35, and 36, White uses each of the three ways to get out of check.

Diagram 35. *The White Bishop blocked the Black Rook to get the White King out of check.*

Diagram 36. *White moved the King to get out of check.*

It isn't necessary to say "check" to your opponent when you attack his or her King. Experienced players never say "check" during a game. Sometimes, though, your opponent might not notice that his or her King is in check. Or when you get *very* skilled at chess, your opponent might think that he or she is moving the King out of check only to find that *another* piece is attacking the King—and that the King is *still* in check! So sometimes you do have to say "check" to prevent your opponent from making an illegal move. Leaving the King in check is illegal.

Likewise, you are never allowed to make a move that places your own King in check: you cannot put the King under the attack of an enemy piece or move it to a square next to the enemy King. That would be illegal. If you accidently place your King in check you must take the move back and make a move that doesn't place your King in check.

At a school chess presentation I asked the class, "What must be done if an illegal move is made?" One of the students replied, "I know what illegal is, an illegal is a sick bird!" An "ill eagle!"

An illegal move is any move that is not allowed to be played according to the rules. If you discover that an illegal move has been made during your game you must correct it by retracing your steps to the illegal move and start from there with a move that is legal.

You might not remember all of the moves that were played during a game. But if you write your moves down, you will have a permanent record of your game. Later on, I'll explain how to read and write chess moves (in Lesson Five—but don't skip ahead!)

CHECKMATE

When a King is attacked by an enemy piece and there is no way for the King to escape on the next move, it is called "checkmate." Checkmate is the purpose of the game. If a player's King has no escape from attack, then he or she is checkmated and loses the game!

In Diagrams 37 and 38 the White King has been checkmated. Black wins the game in both cases.

Diagram 37. The White King cannot escape the attack by the Black Queen—it is checkmated.

Diagram 38. The White King cannot escape the attack by the Black Rook—it is checkmated.

If your King is under attack by an enemy piece and you are not sure whether it is check or checkmate, remember to ask yourself the three ways to get out of check:

1. Can I capture the piece that is attacking my King?
2. Can I block out the piece that is attacking my King?
3. Can I move my King to a square that is not under attack by an enemy piece?

If the answer to all three questions is no, then you are in checkmate!

Here are the ways that a game is lost:

1. Checkmate.
2. Resigning (giving up).
3. Losing "on time" (only if a chess clock is being used—but you don't need to worry about this yet).
4. Refusing to follow the rules of the game.

Serious tournaments use other rules about losing a game. But we don't need to think about these more complicated rules here.

Beginners should *never* resign and give up their game when they are behind. Even if you are far behind you may still be able to save your game. Your opponent may make a mistake! Once you get to be an advanced player you will learn when you should resign.

CASTLING

Because the King is so important there is a special rule to help you to protect it early in the game. This rule is called "castling."

Castling is the *only* time that you are allowed to move two pieces on the same move. And it is the only time that your King can move more than one square on the same move.

Castling uses both a King and a Rook. You can only castle if you have *never* moved the King or the Rook with which you are going to castle. Also, there can't be any pieces between the King and the Rook. In Diagram 39 White can castle with either Rook.

Castling on the short side (where there are two empty squares between the King and Rook) is called "castling

Diagram 39. The White King can castle with either Rook.

Kingside." On the long side (where there are three empty squares between the King and Rook) it is called "castling Queenside."

There are two steps to either kind of castling. First, the King moves two squares toward the Rook. Second, the Rook moves to the other side of the King. Diagram 40 shows the starting position for castling Kingside. The arrows point to the squares that the King and Rook will move to during castling.

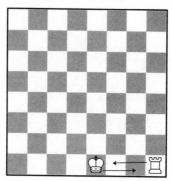

Diagram 40. White is about to castle Kingside.

First the King is moved two squares toward the Rook, reaching the position in Diagram 41.

Diagram 41. *The White King has just moved two squares toward the Rook.*

Then the Rook moves to the square directly on the other side of the King, reaching the position in Diagram 42.

Diagram 42. *White has just completed castling Kingside by moving the Rook to the other side of the King.*

Diagram 43 shows the starting position for castling Queenside. Once again, the arrows show the squares that the King and Rook will move to during castling.

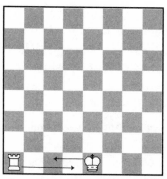

Diagram 43. *The White King is about to castle Queenside.*

Diagram 44. *The White King has just moved two squares toward the Rook.*

Diagram 45. *White has just completed castling Queenside by moving the Rook to the other side of the King.*

First the King moves two squares toward the Rook, reaching the position in Diagram 44.

Then the Rook moves to the square directly on the other side of the King, reaching the position in Diagram 45.

But, remember, you cannot castle if:

1. You have *ever* moved the King or the Rook with which you want to castle. Even if you later move the King or Rook back to its starting square you cannot castle with that piece. But you *can* move one Rook and castle with the *other* Rook.

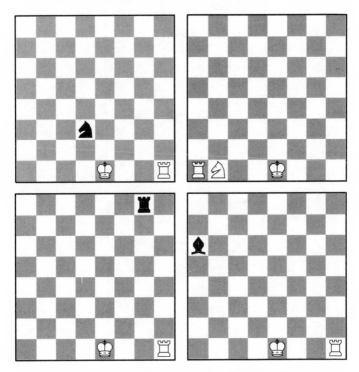

Diagrams 46–49. *Find the reasons why the White King cannot castle in each diagram.*

38

2. There are any pieces between the King and Rook.
3. Your King is in check.
4. Your King must pass over a square that is under attack by an enemy piece.
5. Your King would be in check after you castle.

All of these rules might seem complicated, but you already know most of them. For example, *only* a Knight can jump over another piece: therefore, if there are any pieces between your King and your Rook, they can't jump these pieces. And you can't move your King into check, so obviously it can't pass through a square under attack or move to a square under attack. This should help you remember some of the rules about castling.

In Diagrams 46, 47, 48, and 49 the White King can't castle. See if you can find the reason why in each diagram.

The reasons are:

In Diagram 46 the White King cannot castle because it is in check.

In Diagram 47 the White King cannot castle because there is a piece between it and the Rook.

In Diagram 48 the White King cannot castle because it would be in check after castling.

In Diagram 49 the White King cannot castle because it would pass over a square under attack by an enemy piece.

THE DRAWN GAME

The end result of a game of chess can be a win, a loss, or a draw. A draw in chess is like a tie in most other sports. When the game is drawn there is no winner or loser.

In a chess tournament a player is awarded one point for a win, half a point for a draw, and no points for a loss. Usually at the end of the tournament the player who has scored the most points is the first-place winner. So you can think of a draw as half a win and half a loss!

But for a game to end in a draw doesn't mean that each side has the same amount of "material" (pieces) or the same types of pieces. Many drawn games happen when one side is far ahead of the other.

There are five ways that a game can end in a draw:

1. Stalemate.
2. Insufficient checkmating material (not enough material on the board for either side to checkmate the opponent).
3. Repeating the position three times.
4. Using the fifty-move rule.
5. The two players agree to draw.

These all might seem a little mysterious, so I'll explain them one by one.

STALEMATE

A game ends in a stalemate when the player whose turn it is to move is *not* in check but cannot make a legal move. A stalemate ends the game in a draw.

In Diagrams 50 and 51 it is White's turn to move. There are no legal moves to make and the White King is not in check.

Diagrams 50–51. *White has no legal move to make and is not in check—White has been stalemated in both diagrams.*

41

If the player who's turn it is to move has any piece that he can legally move, then it is *not* a stalemate. In Diagram 52 White has one Pawn that can move, so it is not stalemate.

Diagram 52. White is not stalemated because the Pawn can move.

If you are far behind in material, and things seem lost, you have one hope left—a stalemate! A player who gets far ahead in material must be careful not to stalemate the opponent.

The word "stalemate" is sometimes incorrectly used to mean other types of draws. Use the word "stalemate" only to mean a draw in which a player cannot make a legal move.

INSUFFICIENT MATING MATERIAL

Where there is not enough material on the board for either side to checkmate the opponent, it's called a draw by insufficient mating material. If a player has enough material to checkmate his opponent then this type of draw can't happen. This draw *only* occurs when there are very few pieces left on the board.

Here are some examples of this type of draw:

1. Each player has only a King left on the board.
2. One player has only a King and a Knight and the other player has only a King.
3. One player has only a King and a Bishop and the other player has only a King.

In each of these examples, checkmate is impossible.

REPETITION OF POSITION

If the *exact same* position is repeated three or more times, then the player whose turn it is to make a move can claim a draw. This is called the "repetition of position" draw. Chess games can take a long time to play, but no one wants a game to go on *forever!* That's what this rule is for.

But before you claim this draw, remember:

1. It must be your move. You cannot claim this draw when it is your opponent's turn to move.
2. Both player's pieces must be in the exact same positions—the same squares at the same time—for it to count as a repetition.
3. All of the same *legal* moves must be available to the pieces for each repetition.

The same moves don't have to be made consecutively— that is, from one turn to the next. If the same position occurs at *any* time during the game then it counts as a repetition. Also, if you are about to repeat the position a third time, you may claim the draw before making the move.

THE FIFTY-MOVE RULE

If fifty moves go by without any piece being captured or without any Pawn being moved, the player whose turn it is to move can claim a draw. This is known as the "fifty-move rule." (It's impossible to claim this draw without a written record of the game.)

Just like "repetition of position," this rule prevents a game from going on forever.

Use this rule, for example, if your opponent has only a King and a Rook (or Queen) and you have only your King. Your opponent will then have fifty moves in which to checkmate your King before a draw can be claimed.

DRAW BY AGREEMENT

In tournament games a "draw by agreement" is the most common type of draw. If you want to offer a draw to your opponent you should make the offer immediately after making a move. Your opponent can accept your offer *until* he touches one of his or her pieces. But a beginning-level player won't learn much by accepting or offering a draw early in the game.

Before we go any further, you need to know how to read and write the "chess language." It looks a little like a secret code, but it's easy to learn.

NOTATION: READING AND WRITING CHESS MOVES

As you continue to learn how to play chess, you need to learn how to read chess moves. "Notation" is the code that describes chess moves and positions.

If you start playing in tournaments you'll need to be able to write your moves down. Doing so will give you a permanent record of your game. This will help:

1. Settle questions and disagreements that may come about during the game.
2. Help to improve your game by allowing you to study it.

The most common and easiest type of chess notation to learn is the "algebraic" system. I use the algebraic system in this book. Older chess books use the "descriptive" system of notation. (I'll discuss descriptive notation briefly at the end of the last lesson.)

Each square in the algebraic system has its own name. Let's see how the squares are named.

Each rank (the left-to-right, horizontal rows of squares) has a name. They are numbered from the first rank to the eighth rank. The first rank is at the "bottom" of the board, where you set up the White pieces at the beginning of the game. You always set up the White pieces on the first and

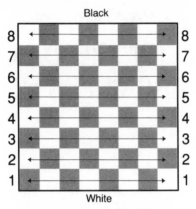

Diagram 53. The ranks are numbered from the first rank to the eighth rank.

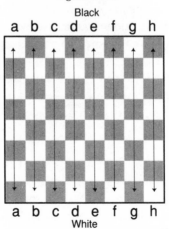

Diagram 54. The files are lettered from the "a" file to the "h" file.

second ranks; the Black pieces are set up on the seventh and eighth ranks. The names of the ranks are shown in Diagram 53.

Each file (the up-and-down, vertical rows of squares) has a name. The ranks are *lettered* from the "a" file to the "h" file. The "a" file is on White's left-hand side. The names of the files are shown in Diagram 54.

By putting together the names of the ranks and the files we get the names of the squares as shown in Diagram 55.

8	a8	b8	c8	d8	e8	f8	g8	h8
7	a7	b7	c7	d7	e7	f7	g7	h7
6	a6	b6	c6	d6	e6	f6	g6	h6
5	a5	b5	c5	d5	e5	f5	g5	h5
4	a4	b4	c4	d4	e4	f4	g4	h4
3	a3	b3	c3	d3	e3	f3	g3	h3
2	a2	b2	c2	d2	e2	f2	g2	h2
1	a1	b1	c1	d1	e1	f1	g1	h1
	a	b	c	d	e	f	g	h

Diagram 55. *Each square has its own name.*

Diagram 55 shows the square in White's lower left-hand corner—"a1." The square directly in front of "a1" is called "a2," and so on, up to the "a8" square.

Once during a school chess presentation one student yelled out, "You sunk my battleship!" If you have ever played the game Battleship, you know that the squares are named the same way. If you buy a chessboard, it's best to get one with algebraic letters and numbers printed around the edges.

Each Pawn is named for the file it begins on. The Pawn on the "a" file is called the "a" Pawn, the Pawn on the "b" file is called the "b" Pawn, and so on—all the way to the

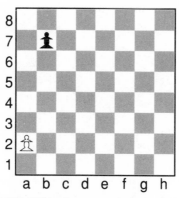

Diagram 56. *The White Pawn is called an "a" Pawn and the Black Pawn is called a "b" Pawn.*

"h" Pawn. Diagram 56 shows a White "a" Pawn and a Black "b" Pawn.

In order to make reading and writing chess moves easier shortcuts or "abbreviations" are used. The abbreviated name for each piece is:

Abbreviated Name	Name of Piece
N	Knight
B	Bishop
R	Rook
Q	Queen
K	King

You'll notice two things. First, there is no abbreviation for the Pawn. Whenever a move just has the name of a square, it means that the move was a Pawn move. Second, "Knight" is abbreviated with "N," even though it begins with a "K." But "King" also begins with a "K," and the King is more important, so it gets its own letter. But it's easy to remember, because the first *sound* of "Knight" is "N"—so that's its letter.

Symbols are also used to explain moves. Some of the symbols are:

Symbol	Meaning
x	captures
+	check
+ +	checkmate
=	promoted to a
0–0	castles Kingside
0–0–0	castles Queenside
e.p.	en passant
?	weak move
??	very weak move (a blunder)
!	strong move
!!	*very* strong move

Some of these symbols aren't used in this book, but they are important to know. You'll need to know them for future games. Let's try to note the moves for a sample game:

Now you definitely need to set up a chessboard. To begin the game, the board is set up with all of the pieces on their starting squares in Diagram 57.

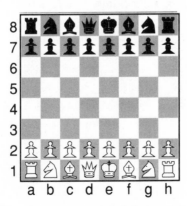

Diagram 57. The pieces are set up and the game is ready to begin!

49

White's first move is *1 e4*. Remember, when no piece abbreviation (like "N," for example) is given, it means that a Pawn moved. So 1 e4 means: For the first move (that's the 1) the "e" Pawn moved from its starting square at e2 to the fourth square in its file (e4). This is the position in Diagram 58.

Diagram 58. *Position after White played 1 e4.*

Now, since the rank numbers start from the White side of the board, when a White Pawn moves forward the numbers get bigger: the White Pawn moved from e2 to e4. But Black moves in the opposite direction, so when a Black Pawn moves forward the numbers get *smaller*.

Black now plays *1 . . . e5*. Black just moved his Pawn from the e7 square to the e5 square, reaching the position in Diagram 59. The three dots (. . .) are used when the Black move is given without the White move being shown before it. This way you can tell immediately after the move number whether it's a White or a Black move. The entire first move—for both White and Black—is written like this: 1 e4 e5. (It's Black's first move too, so it's also "1.").

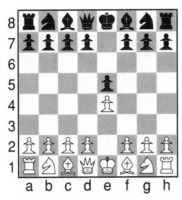

Diagram 59. Position after Black played 1 . . . e5.

White now plays *2 Nf3*: the White Knight moves from its starting square (g1) to the f3 square, reaching the position in Diagram 60. You'll see that after the move number (2), the piece is noted first and then the name of the square it moves to. The abbreviation for the piece is always shown by a capital (upper-case) letter, like "N."

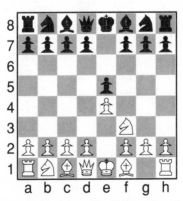

Diagram 60. Position after White played 2 Nf3.

Black now plays *2 . . . Nc6*. Black has just moved his Knight from b8 to c6. This is the position in Diagram 61.

51

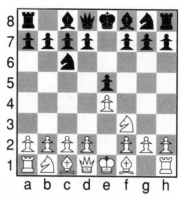

Diagram 61. Position after Black played 2 . . . Nc6.

White now plays *3 Bb5*. White has just moved his Bishop
from f1 to b5. This reaches the position in Diagram 62.

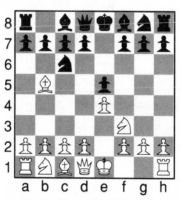

Diagram 62. Position after White played 3 Bb5.

Now a move from each side is shown, *3 . . . a6 4 Bxc6*.
This is a little more complicated, so I'll translate it. On
Black's third move (3 . . . a6), the Black Pawn moves from
a7 (its starting square) to a6; then, on White's fourth move
(4 Bxc6), the White Bishop (B) captures (x) the piece on
c6—a Black Knight. You see how simple algebraic notation
is! Now we're at Diagram 63.

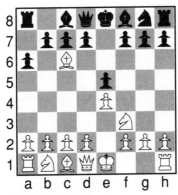

Diagram 63. *Position after 3 ... a6 4 Bxc6.*

When a capture is made *by any piece other than a Pawn:* first, the name of the piece is given; second, the letter "x" shows that a capture was made; and third, the square that the capture is made on is shown.

Black will now capture the Bishop on c6 with the Pawn on d7 by playing *4 ... dxc6.* Just the name of the file that the Pawn *was* on is given when a Pawn makes a capture. The position in Diagram 64 is reached.

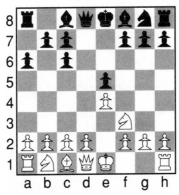

Diagram 64. *Position after 4 ... dxc6.*

White now castles Kingside: *5 0–0.* This is the position in Diagram 65.

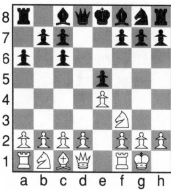

Diagram 65. *Position after White castles Kingside with 5 0–0.*

What happens if two pieces of the same type can move to the same square? How is the difference between the two pieces noted? In Diagram 66 two Knights can move to e2.

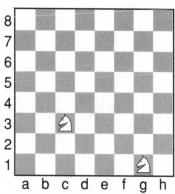

Diagram 66. *White can move either Knight to e2—how is this written?*

The name of the file that the piece is moving *from* is shown. If White wants to move the Knight from g1 to e2 it would be shown as Nge2: the Knight (N) on file "g" moves to e2.

If the Knight in Diagram 66 were on g3 instead of c3, both of the Knights would be on the same file. In that case the name of the *rank* that the piece is moving from is shown. Moving the Knight from g1 to e2 would then be: N1e2.

In Diagram 67 White plays Re1 + . Because this move puts the Black King in check, the symbol + is given at the *end* of the notation.

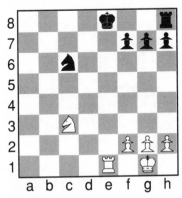

Diagram 67. *White has just put the Black King in check with Re1 + .*

In Diagram 68 White can advance his "d" Pawn to d8 and get a Queen. It would be written down as d8 = Q.

Diagram 68. *White could Queen his Pawn with d8 = Q.*

55

6

INTRODUCTION TO BASIC STRATEGY

Now you know the basic rules of chess. It's time to learn strategy. In order to play a good game of chess you need to have a goal in mind and have reasons for every move you make.

In the first lesson you learned that the final goal in chess is to checkmate the enemy King. You should not expect to be able to do that quickly. As in a real battle, you must first weaken the enemy army, and this may take time. After the enemy has been weakened, you can go in for the final kill.

The most common way to weaken the enemy army is to capture enemy pieces. Be willing to sacrifice your weaker pieces in order to capture your opponent's stronger pieces. The player with more material usually has the advantage and should win the game.

As you plan your battle you should learn how to use strategy. A well-prepared player is difficult to beat. Take time to think over your moves carefully before you act—sit on your hands! Many games are lost because a player acts too quickly and makes a careless move.

The first moves of a game of chess are called the "opening." At the beginning your army is trapped behind a wall of Pawns, and it is important to learn how to get your pieces into play. But you must also keep your King safe.

After your pieces have been brought into play you reach the "middlegame." This is the period of the most intense fighting.

After most of the smoke has cleared and there are few pieces left on the board you have reached the "endgame." At this stage of the game your King is usually brought into play as an active fighting piece. One of the major goals in the endgame is to get a Pawn to the other side of the board and promote it to a Queen.

If mistakes are made a game of chess can be won or lost at any point. Sometimes the middlegame or endgame is never even reached.

INTRODUCTION TO THE OPENING

The first moves of a game are the opening. You are usually in the opening until most, if not all, of your pieces have

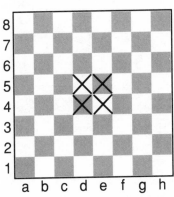

Diagram 69. The four center squares are important to control in the opening.

been brought into play. The opening may last for the first ten to twenty moves of a game.

Two of the major goals in the opening are to get your pieces into play quickly and to control the center of the board. The center four squares of the board (marked "X") are shown in Diagram 69.

Bringing out your pieces in the opening is called "development." Developing your pieces correctly is *very* important. As you develop your pieces toward the center you will control more squares.

I'll show you how moving a piece toward the center increases the number of squares it can attack. You'll see in Diagram 70 that a Knight in its starting position can attack only three squares.

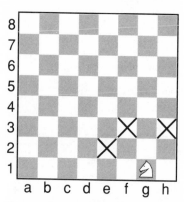

Diagram 70. The Knight can attack only three squares (marked "X") from its starting position.

In Diagram 71 the Knight has been developed to the edge of the board where it can attack only four squares (marked "X").

As you see, developing a Knight to the edge of the board only increases the number of squares it can attack by one. Remember, "A Knight on the rim is dim, its chances are

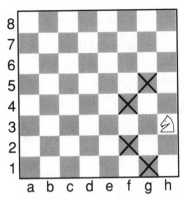

Diagram 71. From the edge of the board the Knight can attack only four squares.

very slim!" Don't develop your Knight to the edge of the board—it may get edgy there!

If you develop your Knight toward the center of the board you can attack *eight* squares (marked "X"), as shown in Diagram 72.

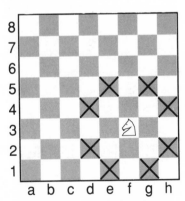

Diagram 72. The Knight can attack eight squares by moving toward the center.

By bringing your Knight out toward the center you get more horsepower out of it!

GENERAL GUIDELINES FOR THE OPENING

To help you better understand the strategy in the opening, here is a list of things to do and *not* to do. These are called "opening principles."

Things to Do in the Opening:

1. Control the center of the board with your pieces.
2. Castle your King early in the game.
3. Develop your Knights and Bishops quickly.
4. Use your two center Pawns ("d" and "e" Pawns) to help control the center.

Things *Not* to Do in the Opening:

1. Do not make a lot of Pawn moves (especially with the "a" and "h" Pawns) without a good reason.
2. Do not keep moving the same piece when you have not developed your other pieces.
3. Do not bring your Queen out too early.

These are just general guidelines. You should use them when you can. They don't apply to every situation. For example, if you can bring your Queen out early and force checkmate on the enemy King quickly, you have a good reason to break a general guideline!

ROLES OF THE PIECES IN THE OPENING

Below is a list of general principles to help you use your pieces effectively in the opening.

THE PAWN

Move your center Pawns ("e" and "d" Pawns) to help control the center and to free your Bishops. (Remember, a

Bishop *can't* jump over other pieces, so you must move at least one of your "b," "d," "e," or "g" Pawns out in order to clear the path for a Bishop.) But don't move out too many Pawns: once a Pawn moves forward, it can never retreat! It usually isn't good to move out the Pawns on the edges ("a" and "h" Pawns) too early in the game.

After you castle it is not good to advance the Pawns in front of the castled King (unless there is a good reason). These Pawns shield the King; when they're moved out, they're less able to protect the King.

THE KNIGHT

The Knight is one of the best pieces to develop quickly toward the center. If you look back at Diagram 72, you'll see that the most powerful squares to develop your Knights to are f3 and c3 (if you are White), and f6 and c6 (if you are Black).

THE BISHOP

The Bishop is also a good piece to develop quickly toward the center. However, don't be too anxious to develop your Bishops deep into enemy territory. They can be easily attacked or captured.

The Knights and Bishops are known as the "minor pieces." I always teach students how important it is to develop their minor pieces quickly.

THE ROOK

The Rook usually isn't active in the opening. Bring it out slowly and use it on "open files." (We'll learn about this later.) In the center of the board the Rook can also be easily attacked by your opponent's weaker pieces.

THE QUEEN

Do not bring it out too early either. Many beginners are tempted to bring out their Queen early because it is so powerful. Your opponent will try as hard as possible to capture your Queen, and you don't want it to be captured by a weaker piece.

THE KING

The King is *the very worst piece* to bring out in the opening. It needs protection. Castling early will usually help protect it.

AN EXAMPLE OF DEVELOPING YOUR PIECES IN THE OPENING

Most openings have a name. Now it's time to learn one called the "Giuoco Piano" (pronounced "joe-ko piano"). It means "slow (or quiet) game" in Italian. In this opening both sides develop their Knights and Bishops very early in order to help control the center.

1 e4

This first move is best if you're a beginning- or intermediate-level player. Moving a Pawn toward the center releases the White Bishop on f1 and the Queen on d1. Freeing your Bishops in the opening by moving center Pawns is very important.

1 . . . e5

Black plays the same move, and gets the same benefits!

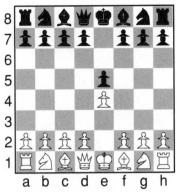

Diagram 73. Position after 1 ... e5.

2 Nf3

White develops a Knight toward the center and attacks the Black Pawn on e5.

2 ... Nc6

Black develops a Knight toward the center and defends the Pawn on e5. Now White wouldn't dare play Nxe5 because Black would play 3 ... Nxe5: White would have captured a Black Pawn, but would have lost a *Knight*, which—if you remember—is worth three Pawns.

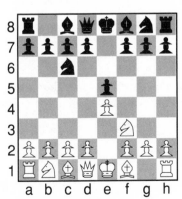

Diagram 74. Position after 2 ... Nc6.

3 Bc4

White develops a Bishop to the long a2–g8 diagonal, where it puts pressure on the Black "f" Pawn—that is, it attacks the Pawn. In the opening the Pawns on f2 and f7 are defended only by the King. This often makes them targets for an attack.

3 . . . Bc5

Black also develops a Bishop to an active position, from which it covers two long diagonals.

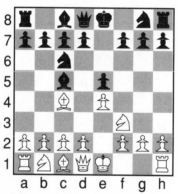

Diagram 75. Position after 3 . . . Bc5.

4 Nc3

White develops a Knight toward the center, continuing to bring out the minor pieces (Knights and Bishops) very quickly.

4 . . . Nf6

Black also develops a Knight and attacks the center.

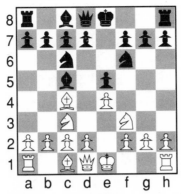

Diagram 76. *Position after 4 . . . Nf6.*

5 d3

By moving the "d" Pawn out, White frees the Bishop on the c1–h6 diagonal and defends the Bishop on c4 *and* the Pawn on e4. (This is very important: Now that the White Pawn on e4 has two pieces protecting it, White has more freedom to move either of the protecting pieces without endangering the Pawn.)

5 . . . d6

Black also frees a Bishop and defends the pieces on c5 and e5.

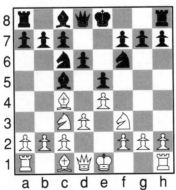

Diagram 77. *Position after 5 . . . d6.*

6 Be3

White develops a Bishop toward the center and challenges the Black Bishop on c5. If Black now captures the White Bishop with 6 . . . Bxe3, White would recapture the Black Bishop with 7 fxe3.

6 . . . Bb6

Black now has his Bishop defended by the "a" Pawn. If White now captures the Black Bishop with 7 Bxb6, Black can capture toward the center with 7 . . . axb6 and open up the "a" file for his or her Rook. As a general rule in the opening it is good to capture *toward* the center with your Pawns.

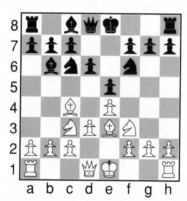

Diagram 78. *Position after 6 . . . Bb6.*

7 Qd2

It would have been legal to castle on the Kingside. However, this move prepares for White to castle on the Queenside. White's Queen is still safe on d2; and because it's closer to the center, it is more active.

7 ... Be6

Black develops the other Bishop, challenging the White Bishop on c4.

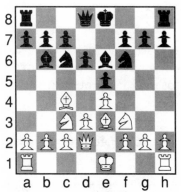

Diagram 79. Position after 7 ... Be6.

8 Bb3

White defends the Bishop with the "a" Pawn. Now if Black captured the Bishop with 8 ... Bxb3, White could recapture toward the center with 9 axb3 and open up the "a" file for the Rook.

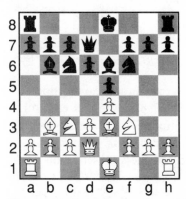

Diagram 80. Position after 8 ... Qd7.

8 . . . Qd7

Black also prepares to castle on the Queenside while bringing the Queen to a safe square.

9 0–0–0

White castles Queenside, moving the King to a safer place. The Rook is now in a more active location. The Pawns in front of the King protect it.

9 . . . 0–0–0

Black also castles to protect the King and activate the Rook.

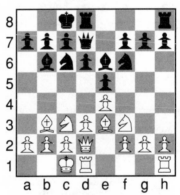

Diagram 81. Position after 9 . . . 0–0–0.

Both sides are in symmetrical positions. This means that the Black and White pieces mirror each other on the board (a copy-cat position). This doesn't happen often in games played by advanced players.

Once at a school chess presentation, I explained a symmetrical position to the class. When I returned the following year to teach the class again I asked them if they remembered what this position is called. One of the kids raised his hand and said, "I remember what you call it—a cemetery position!" You might say he made a "grave" error when he said that!

In the example of the opening that was just given you'll notice that:

1. All of the Knights and Bishops were developed very quickly.
2. The center Pawns were moved to control the center and to free the Bishops.
3. Both sides castled to protect their King and activate a Rook.

These are all very important if you want to play strategically—and if you want to win, that's the best way to play!

INTRODUCING THE HANGING PIECE, THE FORK, AND THE PIN

As I mentioned earlier, one of your major goals is to capture your opponent's material. You should try to win enemy pieces and be willing to trade your weaker pieces for the opponent's stronger pieces. There are some very common patterns (similar types of moves) that can be used to win material. Let's take a look at some common ways that material can be won.

THE HANGING PIECE

When two beginners sit down to play their first game of chess they usually make moves that place their unguarded pieces under attack by enemy pieces. When your opponent can capture an unguarded piece for free it is called a "hanging" piece.

It won't be very long before you learn not to give away pieces for free! And you certainly shouldn't hope that your opponent gives you free pieces and *let* you win!

In Diagrams 82 and 83 see if you can find the Black piece that is hanging.

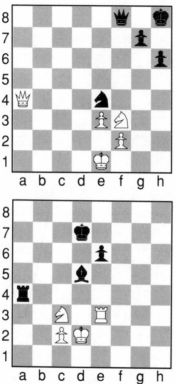

Diagrams 82–83. In each diagram, find the unguarded Black piece that White can capture for free.

In Diagram 82 White can win a free Knight with *1 Qxe4*. In Diagram 83 White can win a free Rook with *1 Nxa4*.

Look before you leap! Before making a move check to see if any enemy pieces are attacking the square where you plan to move. Whenever your opponent makes a move, see if the piece that has just been moved is attacking any of your pieces. Even an advanced player is capable of hanging a piece!

THE FORK

In chess you don't use a fork to eat with! The fork is one of the greatest and most common attacking moves used in chess. Everyone who has played chess seriously has won and lost games because of a fork.

A "fork" is a type of attack in which one piece attacks and threatens two or more enemy pieces at the same time (a double attack). But it's only a fork when *both* of the attacked enemy pieces cannot be protected or when at least one of the attacked pieces is higher in value than the piece that is attacking them.

When a fork is used, the enemy must lose at least one of the threatened pieces. *Any* piece can fork. Pawns, Knights, and Queens are known for their ability to fork. However, the Bishop, Rook, and King are also capable of forking. Let's look at some examples of the fork.

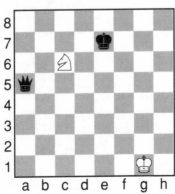

Diagram 84. The White Knight is forking the Black King and Queen.

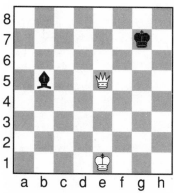

Diagram 85. The White Queen is forking the Black King and Bishop.

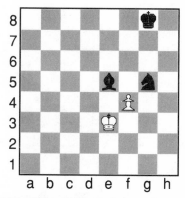

Diagram 86. The White Pawn is forking the Black Knight and Bishop.

In Diagrams 84, 85 and 86 Black must lose a piece because White threatens two pieces at the same time. Black can save only one of the two threatened pieces. It is also possible to use a fork that attacks and threatens *three or more* enemy pieces at the same time!

Let's see if you can find the forks in Diagrams 87, 88, and 89. It is White's turn to move in each of the positions.

73

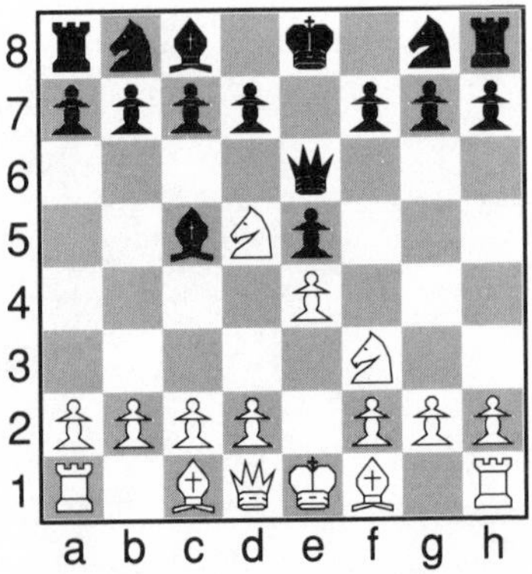

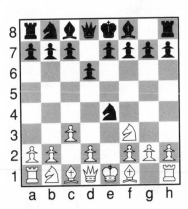

Diagram 87. White can use a Knight fork.

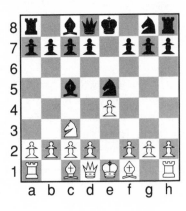

Diagram 88. White can use a Queen fork.

Diagram 89. White can use a Pawn fork.

In Diagram 87 White can fork a King, Queen, and Rook with *1 Nxc7+*. After the Black King moves out of check, White can capture the Black Queen with the Knight. The c7 and c2 squares are squares from which a Knight can very often fork early in the game. This is because only the Queen guards the "c" Pawn at the beginning of the game. Keep this in mind—sooner or later you will see a Knight fork on c7 or c2 in your own games.

In Diagram 88 White can fork a King and Knight with *1 Qa4+*. After the Black King gets out of check, White can capture the Black Knight with 2 Qxe4. The Queen is a very powerful forking piece because it can attack in many directions at the same time!

In Diagram 89 White can fork a Knight and Bishop with *1 d4.* Black must lose either the attacked Knight or Bishop. If Black tries capturing the White Pawn with 1 . . . Bxd4, then White can capture the Black Bishop with 2 Qxd4. The Pawn can never attack more than two pieces at the same time. However, because the Pawn is the weakest of the pieces, you should be willing to trade it for *any* more powerful piece. *This* is what makes the Pawn such a dangerous forking piece.

THE PIN

In chess the "pin" is mightier than the sword! The pin is a common tactic used to win material. Besides being used to win material, the pin can also be used to tie down enemy forces—that is, prevent them from moving.

A pin is an attack on a piece that screens a second piece from attack. You use this move to attack an enemy piece that is unable to move without exposing the piece behind it—usually a more valuable piece—to attack. This may sound a bit complicated, so let's use the example in Diagram 90 for a demonstration!

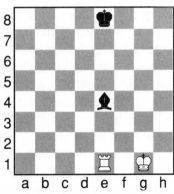

Diagram 90. *The Black Bishop is pinned by the White Rook on the "e" file.*

In Diagram 90 the Bishop can't move because it would put the Black King in check (which would be illegal). Pinning a piece "freezes" it so that your opponent either won't or can't move it.

A pin attacks an enemy piece that has another piece lined up with it on a rank, file, or diagonal. Two enemy pieces must be involved. They must be lined up on the same rank, file or diagonal. Diagram 91 shows a pin on a rank: the Black Knight is pinned by the White Queen.

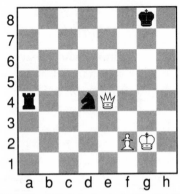

Diagram 91. *The Black Knight is pinned by the White Queen— moving the Knight would allow the Black Rook to be captured.*

76

Just because a piece is pinned doesn't *always* mean that the piece is lost. It may be unable to move, but it may also be protected, as in Diagram 91.

Moving a pinned piece is not allowed if it would expose a King to attack, because you can't put your own King in check. This is called an "absolute pin." Diagram 90 shows an absolute pin.

If moving a pinned piece is legal, but would lose material, it is called a "relative pin." Diagram 91 shows a relative pin.

The three pieces that can pin enemy pieces are the Bishop, Rook, and Queen. A Pawn, Knight, or King cannot pin an enemy piece because of the way they move. (If you try to arrange a setup using one of these pieces to pin, you'll see why they can't do it!)

In Diagram 92 the Black Knight on f6 is pinned by the White Bishop.

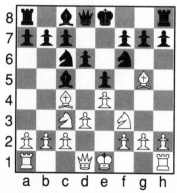

Diagram 92. The Black Knight on f6 cannot move without exposing the Queen to capture—the Knight is pinned.

Let's see if you can find the move that pins a piece in Diagrams 93, 94, and 95. It is White's turn to move in each of the positions.

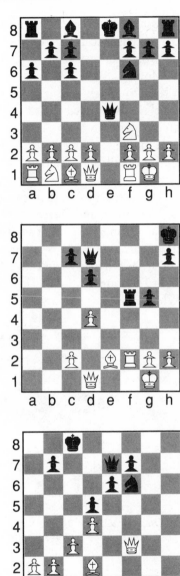

Diagrams 93–95. *It's White's turn. Find the move that pins a Black piece in each Diagram.*

In Diagram 93 White pins the Black Queen with *1 Re1*. The Queen cannot move off the "e" file without placing the King in check. This is an example of an "absolute pin."

In Diagram 94 White pins the Black Rook with *1 Bg4*. The Rook cannot move without placing the Queen under attack by the Bishop. This is an example of a "relative pin."

In Diagram 95 White pins the Black Knight with *1 Bg5*. The Knight is lost because it is attacked by more pieces than defend it. Moving it would expose the Black Queen to attack by the Bishop.

Every experienced chess player has won and lost games because of a pin!

THE DUMB COMPUTER

The kids I teach love to play against a computer. They call it the "Dumb Computer" because it was programmed to bring out its Queen too early.

The kids know that if they get the computer to bring out its Queen too early, they can capture the Queen and beat the computer. When they go home, they all tell their parents, "I beat a computer at chess." Before long everyone thinks that the kids are *great* chess players—but they never told their parents that they played against a *dumb* computer!

Let's take a look at how the kids won the Dumb Computer's Queen. This example shows the pin and fork in action. You can use a chess set to follow the moves.

The students play White and the Dumb Computer plays Black.

1 e4 d5

The Dumb Computer is playing an opening called the "Center-Counter Defense." (The moves played in the open-

79

ing of a game usually have a name. The name of the opening helps you to identify the early moves played in a game.)

The Center-Counter Defense isn't very good for Black.
Only the Black Queen is defending the Pawn on d5. Let's
see how the students take advantage of this.

2 exd5

White is going to use a Pawn as bait for the Black Queen.
The students know that the computer is very greedy and
likes to take things that look free!

2 . . . Qxd5

The Dumb Computer brings its Queen out early to capture the Pawn. Now the students can use the Black Queen
as a target. The position in Diagram 96 is reached.

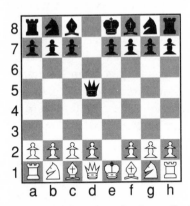

Diagram 96. *Position after 2 . . . Qxd5.*

3 Nc3

The Knight is developed toward the center and gains
time by attacking the Black Queen.

3 . . . Qc6??

(Remember, ? means a weak move, and ?? means a very weak move.) This move will lose the Black Queen. It would have been better for the Dumb Computer to return the Queen home with 3 . . . Qd8. The position in Diagram 97 is reached. See if you can find a pin that will capture the Black Queen in two moves.

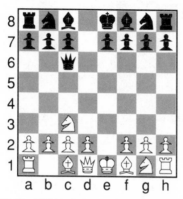

Diagram 97. Find White's move that pins the Black Queen.

3 Bb5

The Dumb Computer's Queen has been pinned. It cannot move off the a4–e8 diagonal because that would place the Black King in check. The White Knight on c3 is defending the Bishop on b5. What can the Dumb Computer do to save the Queen? Nothing. The Dumb Computer decides at least to capture a Bishop for its lost Queen.

3 . . . Qxb5 4 Nxb5 a6??

This move is very weak because it allows a Knight fork. See if you can find the move for White that forks a King and Rook in Diagram 98.

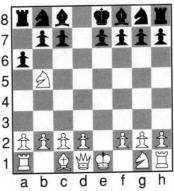

Diagram 98. Find the move for White that forks the Black King and Rook.

5 Nxc7+

The King and Rook are attacked at the same time. Black must get the King out of check.

5 . . . Kd8 6 Nxa8

White is far ahead in material and should win the game! Let's look at an example of how a pin and fork can work together to capture a Queen. In Diagram 99 White first

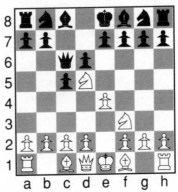

Diagram 99. White can use a pin and fork to win the Black Queen.

uses a pin to force the Black Queen to a square where it is
set up for a Knight fork. See if you can find White's move.

White first uses a pin with *1 Bb5!*. This pins the Black
Queen to the King. The only way for the Black Queen to
get out of attack is to play *1 . . . Qxb5,* reaching the position in Diagram 100. See if you can find a Knight fork
that will capture the Balck Queen in Diagram 100.

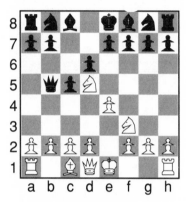

*Diagram 100. Find White's move that will use a fork to win the
Black Queen.*

White plays *2 Nc7+*, forking the King, Queen, and
Rook *at the same time!* You might call this a family fork!
After Black gets his King out of check with *2 . . . Kd8,*
White captures the Queen with *3 Nxb5.*

Now that you've learned some general principles of
strategy (can you remember the opening principles?) and
some basic maneuvers, it's time to move on to the last part
of a chess game.

LESSON

INTRODUCTION TO THE ENDGAME

The endgame is reached when there are very few pieces left on the board. A different kind of strategy is used in the endgame than in the opening or middlegame.

Earlier in the game the King constantly needs protection. In the endgame the King becomes an active fighting piece. At this point it is usually in less danger of being checkmated because there is not a lot of material on the board.

Pawns also take on a very important role in the endgame. The major goal in most endgames is to Queen a Pawn. The winner is often the player who gets a Pawn to the eighth rank first. The player with an extra Queen is almost always able to checkmate the opponent quickly. Being ahead by one Pawn in the endgame can make all the difference.

When studying the endgame you should learn the most basic positions first. Learning how to checkmate a lone

King (a King with no other pieces from its army) with just one or two pieces is the best starting point.

I mentioned earlier that if one player has *only* a King and a Bishop or Knight, and the other has only a King, the game ends in a draw. You must have at least a King and a Rook, or a King, a Bishop, and a Knight, to be able to checkmate a lone King.

One important tip about checkmating a lone King: It is easiest to checkmate the King in a corner or on the edge of the board. Diagram 101 shows how many squares (marked "X") a King can move to from the edge, the center, and the corner of the board.

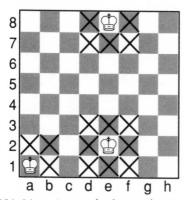

Diagram 101. It's easiest to checkmate the King in a corner.

From Diagram 101 you will see that: the King on a1 can move to only three squares, the King on e8 can move to five squares, and the King on e2 can move to eight squares. Limiting the number of squares that the enemy King can move to will make it much easier to checkmate it. Often the enemy King must be driven to the edge of the board before you can checkmate it. If all you have left is a King and Rook (or Queen) you can *only* checkmate the lone King at an edge or corner of the board.

CHECKMATE WITH TWO ROOKS AND A KING VERSUS A KING

Knowing how to use a "Rook Roller" is a basic endgame checkmating tactic that every beginner should know. You'll win games using it! The Rook Roller can be used with either two Rooks, two Queens, or a Rook and a Queen. When the Rook Roller is used, the two pieces are used to drive the King to the edge of the board, one rank or file with each move.

Let's see if you can find the final move of a Rook Roller from the position given in Diagram 102. It is White's turn to move.

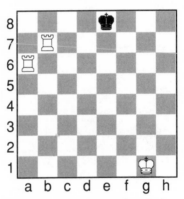

Diagram 102. White can checkmate the Black King in one move.

If you found **1 Ra8 + +**, then you found the checkmate. The Rook on a8 attacks the Black King and covers the entire eighth rank. The Rook on b7 covers the entire seventh rank in front of the Black King. Both Rooks work together to checkmate the Black King.

In Diagram 103 it is White's move. See if you can checkmate Black in two moves using a Rook Roller.

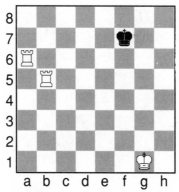

Diagram 103. White can checkmate Black in two moves.

From Diagram 103 White begins with *1 Rb7+*. The Rook drives the King back to the edge of the board. The Rook on a6 covers the sixth rank, which prevents the Black King from going toward the center. The position in Diagram 104 has been reached.

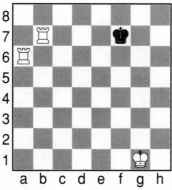

Diagram 104. Black has nothing better than to retreat with 1 . . . Ke8.

Black can do nothing better than retreat with *1 . . . Ke8*, allowing checkmate with *2 Ra8+ +*.

Let's look at the Rook Roller that requires three moves to checkmate, as in Diagram 105.

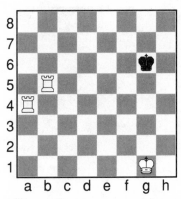

Diagram 105. White to move and checkmate Black in three moves.

(Now that you've gotten used to algebraic notation, I'm not going to illustrate every move. Try the next example on your own, starting from Diagram 105.)

White uses a Rook Roller to drive the Black King and checkmate him with *1 Ra6+ Kf7 2 Rb7+ Ke8 3 Ra8++*.

CHECKMATE WITH A QUEEN AND A KING VERSUS A LONE KING

This is one of the most common and important basic checkmates for a beginner to learn. In order to checkmate a lone enemy King when you have only a King and Queen left on the board, you must use your King actively. The enemy King must be driven to the edge of the board before he can be checkmated.

Let's start out with some simple positions showing where the final checkmate can happen. In Diagram 106 the White Queen can move to five different squares in order to checkmate the Black King. These squares are marked "X."

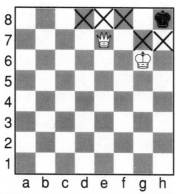

Diagram 106. *White can checkmate the Black King by moving the Queen to a square marked "X."*

You'll notice that the White King must be nearby to assist the Queen with the checkmate.

See if you can find a checkmate in Diagrams 107 and 108. It is White's move in both positions.

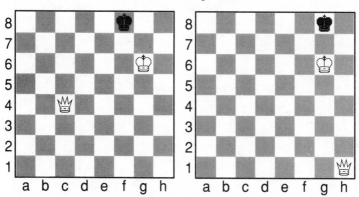

Diagrams 107–108. *White can checkmate Black in one move.*

In Diagram 107 Black is checkmated with *1 Qf7+ +*. The Queen is protected by the White King.

In Diagram 108 Black is checkmated with *1 Qa8+ +*. The Queen attacks along the entire eighth rank. The White

King prevents the Black King from moving off the eighth rank. This is a good example of the long-range powers of the Queen.

In Lesson Ten you'll learn more about how to checkmate a lone King with just your King and Queen. But before you learn in detail how to end a game, you need to learn in detail how to begin one!

LESSON

9

▼▼▼▼▼▼▼▼▼▼▼▼▼▼▼▼

LEARNING AN OPENING SYSTEM

It is important to study the opening and prepare an opening system. If you don't survive the opening, you'll never reach the middlegame or the endgame!

There are many different openings. In order to be a good chess player you don't need to know *all* of the openings. Trying to examine too many openings at the same time can be confusing and will waste valuable time. You should begin by learning just a few openings—but learn them well! Preparing an opening system means studying a small number of openings that you are likely to use.

Stick to the openings in this book. After you know them well you can expand your opening knowledge. Once you learn the ones I'll teach you here, you're on your way to having a well-rounded system.

When you study the opening, don't just memorize moves! It is very important for you to understand why each move is made. And be sure to know whether the opening given in this book is best for White or for Black! A good opening for White may not be the best for Black!

91

INTRODUCTION TO THE RUY LOPEZ

The Ruy (pronounced "roo-ee") Lopez is one of the most famous openings. It is named after a Spanish Bishop by that name who lived in the sixteenth century. One student said, "If you play the Ruy Lopez without knowing it well, you will turn it into a Ruined Lopez!" This is true!

The first two moves of the Ruy Lopez are exactly the same as the Giuoco Piano, covered in the last lesson. Let's look at the opening moves of the Ruy Lopez.

1 e4 e5 2 Nf3 Nc6 3 Bb5

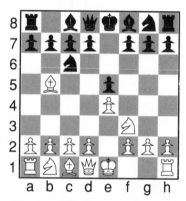

Diagram 109. *Position after 3 Bb5.*

White's third move develops a Bishop with an attack on the Black Knight on c6. Even though the Knight is protected by *two* Pawns, Black must still be careful.

The Knight on c6 defends the Pawn on e5. If White captures the Black Knight with Bxc6, there would be nothing defending the "e" Pawn. This can get tricky, as you'll see in the Exchange Variation of the Ruy Lopez.

THE EXCHANGE VARIATION OF THE RUY LOPEZ

In this variation of the Ruy Lopez, White will exchange the Bishop for the Black Knight on c6. I recommend the Ruy Lopez Exchange Variation for *Black,* but not for White.

1 e4 e5 2 Nf3 Nc6 3 Bb5 a6

This is the most common third move for Black to play against the Ruy Lopez. Black attacks the White Bishop on b5 and will force it either to retreat or to be exchanged for the Knight.

4 Bxc6

White exchanges the Bishop for the Black Knight. This removes an important defender of the Black "e" Pawn, and gives Black "doubled Pawns." (Doubled Pawns are two Pawns of the same color on the same file. They're usually a weakness.)

On the other hand, White is giving up a very active Bishop. This gives Black the "Bishop Pair." Having the

4 . . . dxc6

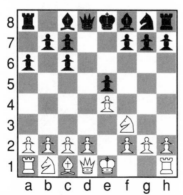

Diagram 110. *Position after 4 . . . dxc6.*

93

Bishop Pair means that one side has two Bishops, while the opponent has either a Knight and a Bishop or two Knights. Usually, having the Bishop Pair is a slight advantage in an open type of position. An open position is one where the pieces have a lot of freedom to move.

Black captures the Bishop while giving the Queen room to move on the "d" file and freeing the Bishop's path on the "c8–h3" diagonal. It is important to free your pieces in the opening.

The Pawns on c6 and c7 are doubled Pawns.

5 0–0

White cannot win a Pawn by playing 5 Nxe5 because Black has a Queen fork with 5 ... Qd4!. If White then saves the attacked Knight with 6 Nf3, Black can recapture the Pawn with 6 ... Qxe4+. The game might continue with 7 Qe2 Qxe2+ 8 Kxe2, and then White will never be able to castle. Therefore, it isn't wise for White to grab a Pawn on move five!

5 ... Bg4

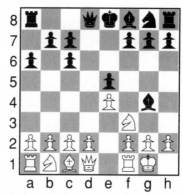

Diagram 111. *Position after 5 ... Bg4.*

Black develops a Bishop and pins the White Knight.

6 h3

The Pawn attacks the Black Bishop.

6 ... h5

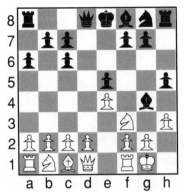

Diagram 112. Position after 6 ... h5.

Black sets up a trap, using the Bishop as bait.

7 hxg4?

White falls for the trap! It is better for White to ignore the Bishop and play 7 d3, freeing some of the Queenside pieces and defending the "e" Pawn. After 7 d3, Black would be smart to increase the attack on the pinned White Knight with 7 ... Qf6. A good plan for Black then would be to develop the Kingside pieces and castle on the Queenside.

7 ... hxg4

Black opens up the Rook on the "h" file and attacks the White Knight on f3.

8 Nxe5?

White is greedy to the end! As you'll soon see, it's better for White to leave the Knight on f3 and save the King. It is *much* better to lose a Knight than a King. The White Knight no longer prevents the Black Queen from going to h4.

8 . . . Qh4!

Black is threatening 9 . . . Qh2 + + or 9 . . . Qh1 + + .

9 f4

White opens up the f2 square for the King. However, with Black's next move there will be *no* escape for the White King!

9 . . . g3!

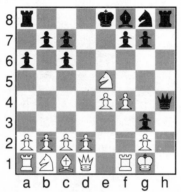

Diagram 113. Position after 9 . . . g3!.

White has no defense against the checkmate threat of Qh1 + + . Be careful not to open up lines of attack against your castled King. If your opponent offers something that looks like it is free, double check to be sure that it isn't a trap!

INTRODUCTION TO THE MAIN LINE OF THE RUY LOPEZ

This is the most common variation that two experienced players will use when playing the Ruy Lopez. The Main Line of the Ruy Lopez is good for both White *and* Black. The first three moves are the same as in the Exchange Variation.

1 e4 e5 2 Nf3 Nc6 3 Bb5 a6 4 Ba4

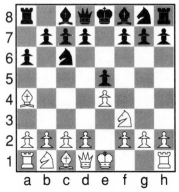

Diagram 114. *Position after 4 Ba4.*

When you are playing White, if your Bishop is attacked you should retreat rather than exchange it. The Bishop still attacks the Black Knight on c6, and it can be shifted to the long "a2–g8" diagonal.

4 . . . Nf6

This develops the Knight to its most active position with an attack on the White "e" Pawn.

5 0–0

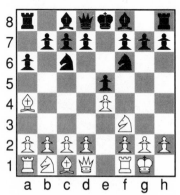

Diagram 115. *Position after 5 0–0.*

White moves the King from the center into safety and activates a Rook. In Lesson Eleven you will see why I recommend that Black develop the Bishop with 5 . . . Be7, rather than grab a Pawn with 5 . . . Nxe4.

Now that you know the most important opening strategies, we can move on to the purpose of a chess game: checkmate!

·····································

BASIC CHECKMATE POSITIONS

Some types of checkmates happen so often that they have names so you can identify them. Learning the patterns used in these checkmates will make you a *much* better player. Let's take a look at some of these checkmates.

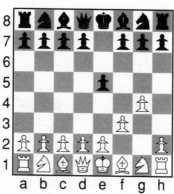

Diagram 116. Position after 2 g4??—Black can checkmate White in one move.

THE FOOL'S MATE

It is possible to win a game in as few as two moves! Here's how. Make these moves:

1 f3? e5 2 g4??

Can you find the checkmate for Black in one move in Diagram 116?

If you found **2 ... Qh4 + +** then you used the Fool's Mate. It is called a Fool's Mate because only a *fool* would make the moves that White made! You're not likely to have these exact moves played against you. However, this type of Queen attack against a King is common along:

1. The "h5–e8" diagonal for a White Queen.
2. The "h4–e1" diagonal for a Black Queen.

This may happen when an "f" Pawn is moved early in the opening.

See if you can find the checkmate for White in two moves in Diagram 117.

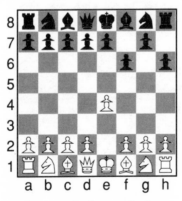

Diagram 117. White can checkmate Black in only two moves.

White checkmates Black in two moves with *1 Qh5 + g6 2 Qxg6 + +*. White has just used the same checkmating pattern that was used in the Fool's Mate.

A Bishop can use the same type of checkmate. In Diagram 118 Black can checkmate White in one move. See if you can find the move.

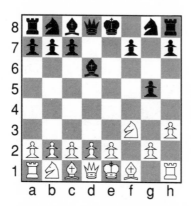

Diagram 118. *Black can checkmate White in one move.*

Black uses the Fool's Mate pattern to checkmate White with *1 . . . Bg3 + +*.

CHECKMATE ON f7 OR f2

At the beginning of the game the f7 and f2 squares are only defended by the King. Often the "f" Pawn becomes a target of attack by enemy pieces. This can sometimes result in an early checkmate.

In Diagram 119 White has a Bishop and Knight attacking the Black "f" Pawn. See if you can find the checkmate for White in one move.

White checkmates Black with *1 Bxf7 + +*.

See if you can find the checkmate for Black in Diagram 120.

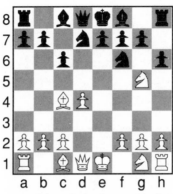

Diagram 119. White can checkmate Black in one move.

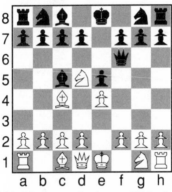

Diagram 120. Black can checkmate White in one move.

Black checkmates White with *1 . . . Qxf2 + +*.

Another very famous checkmate is known as the "Scholar's Mate." This is also sometimes known as the "Four-move checkmate." White will bring out the Queen and Bishop quickly and try to checkmate Black on f7. This may result in a quick checkmate against a beginner. However, it is not a good idea to bring out the Queen too early. With good play, Black will be able to stop the Scholar's Mate and get a good position.

Let's take a look at the moves in Scholar's Mate.

1 e4 e5 2 Qh5

This move brings out the Queen too early, which is not a good idea. The White Queen attacks the Black "f" Pawn and also threatens to capture the "e" Pawn.

2 . . . Nc6

Black defends the "e" Pawn by developing a Knight. Black would not want to play 2 . . . g6??, because White would play 3 Qxe5 +, forking the Black King and Rook.

3 Bc4

White now has *two* pieces attacking the Black "f" Pawn.

3 . . . Nf6??

This blunder allows White to checkmate Black on the next move. See if you can find the checkmate for White in Diagram 121.

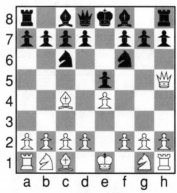

Diagram 121. *Position after 3 . . . Nf6??. Can you find the checkmate for White?*

White checkmates Black with *4 Qxf7+ +*.

Let's look at how Black can stop the Scholar's Mate. We need to go back to Black's third move. Instead of playing 3 . . . Nf6??, Black can play

3 . . . g6

This blocks and attacks the White Queen.

4 Qf3

White threatens to checkmate Black again with 5 Qxf7 + +.

4 . . . Nf6

Black develops his Knight and blocks the Black Queen. Black now has a good game and threatens to post his Knight actively with 5 . . . Nd4, which would attack White's Queen and threaten a fork with 6 . . . Nxc2 +.

THE SMOTHERED MATE

This is one of the most beautiful of all the checkmates. A "Smothered Mate" occurs when a King is completely surrounded by its own pieces and is checkmated by a Knight.

In Diagram 122 White can checkmate Black in one move with a Smothered Mate. See if you can find the move.

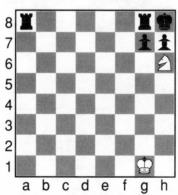

Diagram 122. White to move and use a Smothered Mate in one move.

White checkmates Black with *1 Nf7+ +*. This is the final position from a type of Smothered Mate known as the "Philidor's Legacy" (which I'll discuss in Lesson Fourteen).

A famous game using the Smothered Mate lasted only six moves. Let's take a look.

1 e4 c6 2 d4 d5 3 Nc3 dxe4 4 Nxe4 Nd7 5 Qe2 Ngf6??

This blunder allows White to use a Smothered Mate in one move. Black could have played a move like *5 . . . e6*, which would have stopped the checkmate.

Diagram 123 shows the position after *5 . . . Ngf6??* See if you can find a move for White that uses a Smothered Mate.

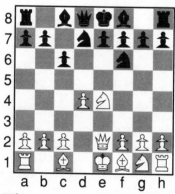

Diagram 123. White to move and checkmate Black in one move.

White checkmates Black with *6 Nd6+ +*. The "e" Pawn cannot capture the Black Knight because the White Queen on e2 pins the Pawn. This checkmate *must* have taken Black by surprise!

THE BACKRANK MATE

One of the most common types of checkmates is the "Backrank Mate." When you castle, you try to place the King behind a protective shield of Pawns. If you're not careful, though, these same Pawns can trap your King. But if your opponent castles, you may be able to trap the enemy King this way!

In a Backrank Mate you attack the King with a Rook or Queen along the last rank (the first rank for White or the eighth rank for Black). The King is blocked from moving forward (to the second or seventh rank) by its own Pawns.

In Diagram 124 White can use a Backrank Mate on Black. See if you can find it.

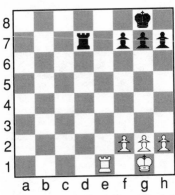

Diagram 124. White can checkmate Black in one move.

White checkmates Black with *1 Re8 + +*. If *any* of the Pawns had moved, the King would have had an escape square. Often a Backrank Mate can be prevented by moving one of the Pawns in front of the King after castling. Making a breathing space for a King in this way is called creating "Luft." ("Luft," pronounced "looft," means "air" in German.)

Creating Luft too early in the game isn't a good idea,

because there is usually no threat of a Backrank Mate in the opening. And moving a Pawn in front of a castled King can sometimes create a weak point.

Keeping a Rook on the first rank (or eighth rank if you are Black) is sometimes not enough protection against a Backrank Mate. In Diagram 125 White can sacrifice the Queen to get a Backrank Mate. See if you can find the checkmate in two moves for White.

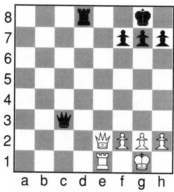

Diagram 125. White can checkmate Black in two moves by sacrificing the Queen.

White checkmates Black in two moves with *1 Qe8+ Rxe8 2 Rxe8+ +*. After you have castled your King, *always* be ready for a Backrank Mate. Every experienced player has both won and lost games because of this important type of checkmate.

CHECKMATE IN THE ENDGAME WITH A QUEEN AND A KING VERSUS A LONE KING

In Lesson Eight you learned the final checkmating positions that use a King and Queen against a lone King. Now you are going to learn how to force a checkmate by pushing your opponent's King to the edge of the board.

But you must be very careful not to stalemate your opponent! See if you can find White's moves in Diagram 126 that will checkmate Black in three moves.

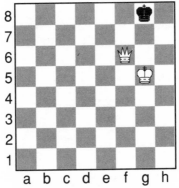

Diagram 126. White can checkmate Black in three moves.

White must be careful not to stalemate Black with 1 Kg6 or 1 Kh6. This would not allow the Black King a legal move and would result in a draw. Let's take a look at the moves that lead to the quickest checkmate.

1 Qe7

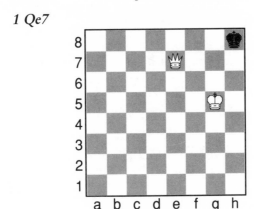

Diagram 127. Position after 1 . . . Kh8.

This move ties the King down to the edge of the board

where you want it. The Black King is left with only one square to move to.

1 . . . Kh8

White can now move the King in for the final kill!

2 Kg6 Kg8 3 Qg7+ +

Or 3 Qe8 or 3 Qd8 would also be checkmate.

In this basic checkmate keep in mind that your King must be an *active* fighting piece. It can help not only by assisting in the final checkmate, but also to drive the enemy King back to the edge of the board.

Let's take a look at an example of how to drive an enemy King from the center of the board to the edge. In Diagram 128 the Black King must be driven from the center to the edge of the board.

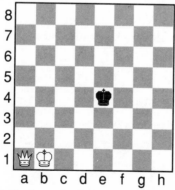

Diagram 128. To force checkmate, White must drive the Black King to the edge of the board.

If you move your King and Queen toward the center of the board, you'll drive the enemy King back! You can begin by moving your King directly into the center from the position in Diagram 128. Let's see how this works.

109

1 Kc2

The White King begins his march toward the center. Black will do his best to keep his King in the center.

1 ... Kd5 2 Kd3 Kc5

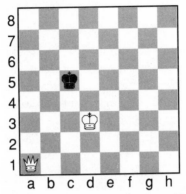

Diagram 129. Position after 2 ... Kc5.

Now that the White King can't get any closer to the enemy King it is time to bring the Queen into the center to help.

3 Qe5 + Kc6

Diagram 130. Position after 3 ... Kc6.

The Black King has already been driven from the center. The White King will continue to move toward the enemy King in order to drive it to the edge of the board.

4 Kc4 Kd7 5 Kc5

The Black King must go to the edge of the board.

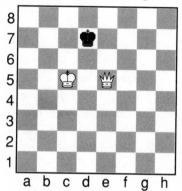

Diagram 131. Position after 5 Kc5.

5 . . . Kc8

White can now tie down the Black King to the edge of the board (the eighth rank in this case) with the next move.

6 Qe7

Diagram 132. Position after 6 Qe7.

The Black King is now trapped on the edge of the board, and the White King will move in to assist with the final kill!

6 ... Kb8 7 Kb6 Kc8 8 Qc7+ +

Or White could have also checkmated Black with 8 Qe8 + +.

You probably haven't noticed, but with each new lesson I've tried to expand a different part of the game so that you know how to play a *whole* game of chess. For example, in Lesson Seven, I showed you basic maneuvers like the fork. In Lesson Eight you learned about the endgame, and in Lesson Nine about opening systems. Since we just covered different kinds of checkmate, now we're going *back* to the opening again—jumping around like a Knight!

If you think back to the very beginning, when you may not have even known what a Pawn is, you'll see how far you've come and how much fun it's been!

11

▼▼▼▼▼▼▼▼▼▼▼▼▼▼▼▼▼▼▼▼

THE OPEN VARIATION OF THE RUY LOPEZ

The first five moves for White are the same as the moves for the Main Line of the Ruy Lopez. (Do you remember them? I talked about them in Lesson Nine.) On the fifth move, though, Black captures the unprotected "e" Pawn. The Pawn may look like it's free—but White has a strong counterattack that will capture a Black Pawn at the very least!

The Open Variation is not recommended for Black. We'll study it from White's point of view. Let's take a look at the moves leading up to the Open Variation.

1 e4 e5 2 Nf3 Nc6 3 Bb5 a6 4 Ba4 Nf6 5 0–0 Nxe4

Black captures the White "e" Pawn, going into the Open Variation of the Ruy Lopez. If you are playing the Ruy Lopez with the Black pieces, you should play 5 . . . Be7. (I'll show you more about this in the next lesson.)

113

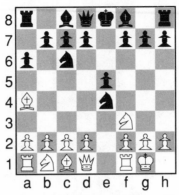

Diagram 133. Position after 5 . . . Nxe4.

6 d4

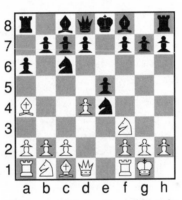

Diagram 134. Position after 6 d4.

White boldly attacks in the center with a Pawn. This does several things:

1. It frees the Bishop on c1.
2. It opens up d2 for use by a Knight.
3. It activates the Queen on the "d" file.

The Black "e" Pawn is now under attack by *two* White pieces, but is defended by only *one* piece. Usually when a

114

piece is attacked by more pieces than are defending it, it's in trouble.

Part of White's plan is to open up the "e" file for the Rook. If White had immediately brought the Rook out with 6 Re1, then the Black Knight would have gone to a good square with 6 . . . Nc5. The Knight would then be threatening the White Bishop on a4.

White tries to get rid of Black's "e" Pawn before attacking on the "e" file with a Rook. You will see shortly why this is important!

6 . . . exd4

It's risky to capture the second Pawn. It's better to force the White Bishop off of the "a4–e8" diagonal with 6 . . . b5 7 Bb3 d5. White then would be able to recapture the Pawn with 8 dxe5.

7 Re1

White now brings the Rook into play on the open "e" file, pinning the Black Knight.

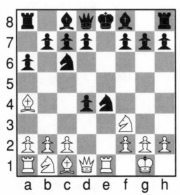

Diagram 135. *Position after 7 Re1.*

7 . . . d5

Black defends the Knight on e4 while freeing the Bishop on c8. However, the Black Knight on c6 is also pinned! Black now has two paralyzed Knights!

8 Nxd4

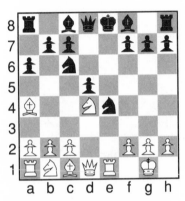

Diagram 136. *Position after 8 Nxd4.*

White wins one of the Pawns back and is attacking the Black Knight on c6 with two pieces—but the Knight is only defended by one piece. The Black Knight on e4 is also in trouble. White threatens to play 9 f3, attacking the pinned Knight on e4.

8 . . . Be7

Black decides to develop a Bishop and "unpin" the Knight on e4. If White plays 9 f3, attacking the Knight, it can now move to c5. However, this doesn't help the Black Knight on c6!

9 Nxc6 bxc6 10 Bxc6 +

Black has been forked! The King, Rook, and Pawn are attacked by the Bishop on c6.

116

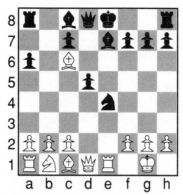

Diagram 137. Position after 10 Bxc6 + .

10 . . . Bd7 11 Bxd5

White captures a free Pawn while forking the White Rook on a8 and the undefended Knight on e4. With threats like this, Black must lose more material!

If Black moves the Knight on e4, then White can play 12 Bxa8, and after 12 . . . Qxa8 White has won a Rook for the Bishop.

When you win a Rook in exchange for a minor piece (a Knight or Bishop) it is called "winning the exchange"; and when you *lose* a Rook in exchange for a minor piece it is called "losing the exchange."

If Black saves the Rook by moving it, then White can capture the Knight on e4.

TACTICAL MOTIFS

You were introduced to some basic tactics in the last two lessons. It is time to expand on some of these ideas and to introduce new tactical motifs. A "motif" (pronounced "moe-teef") is a pattern of moves containing an idea or theme.

ATTACKING THE KING ON THE WEAKENED "h5–e8" AND "h4–e1" DIAGONALS

When we watched the Fool's Mate in the last lesson we used an attack along the weakened "h4–e1" diagonal. Sometimes, it's not obvious how you can take advantage of a weakened "h5–e8" or "h4–e1" diagonal, so you have to think ahead! Sometimes if you sacrifice a piece, you'll checkmate your opponent or win material back—but unless you think ahead, you might sacrifice a piece for nothing.

The first example of a sacrifice using this theme is from an opening known as "From's Gambit." A "gambit" is when you sacrifice a Pawn or other piece in the opening because you hope to get a good position in return for it. But not all gambits are good. In many cases you don't get enough in return for the material that you have given up.

Make the following moves, and see if you can find a checkmate in three moves for Black.

1 f4 e5 2 fxe5 d6 3 exd6 Bxd6 4 Nc3??

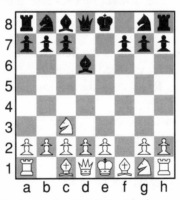

Diagram 138. Position after 4 Nc3??—Black can checkmate White in three moves.

White's last move was a serious blunder. It's better to develop a Knight and defend h4 with 4 Nf3. Let's take a look at the moves that force a checkmate.

4 . . . Qh4+ 5 g3

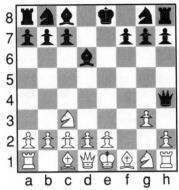

Diagram 139. *Position after 5 g3—Black can checkmate White in two moves.*

In Diagram 139 Black has two ways to force a quick checkmate.

A. *5 . . . Bxg3+! 6 hxg3 Qxg3++* (or)
B. *5 . . . Qxg3+! 6 hxg3 Bxg3++*.

One of the fastest games played lasted only five moves! Here is how it went:

1 d4 Nf6 2 Nd2

This blocks the White Bishop along the "c1–h6" diagonal. A better move is 2 c4. This would help control the center with a Pawn and give White a "Pawn Center." You get a "Pawn Center" when your Pawns are in the center during the opening. That's usually a good idea.

2 . . . e5

Black now plays a gambit (in this case a Pawn sacrifice).

3 dxe5

White now threatens to capture the Black Knight.

119

4 ... Ng4 5 h3??

It's better for White to develop a Knight and defend his "e" Pawn with 5 Ngf3. The move 5 h3?? allows Black to make a fantastic sacrifice, leading to the capture of the White Queen or even a checkmate. Can you see how?

Diagram 140. Position after 5 h3??.

From the position in Diagram 140 Black wins with

5 ... Ne3!!

This attacks the White Queen. If White doesn't capture the Knight the Queen is lost. White resigned here. Let's take a look at how the game might have continued.

6 fxe3

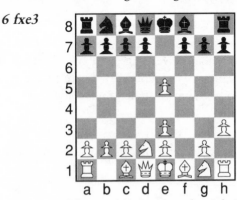
Diagram 141. Position after 6 fxe3.

120

Black can now checkmate White in two moves.

6 . . . Qh4+ 7 g3 Qxg3+ +

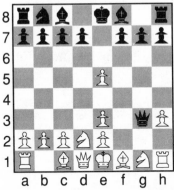

Diagram 142. Position after 7 . . . Qxg3 + +. White has been checkmated!

The following example is taken from an opening known as the "King's Gambit Declined." In the King's Gambit Declined, White offers the sacrifice of the "f" Pawn to remove Black's "e" Pawn from the center and to open the "f" file. But Black doesn't accept the offer!

The position in Diagram 143 is reached after the following moves:

1 e4 e5 2 f4 Bc5 3 fxe5??

Diagram 143. Black can win at least a Rook.

White will lose at least a Rook, so it's better for White to develop a Knight with 3 Nf3. Let's look at Black's winning moves.

3 ... Qh4+ 4 g3

White would be checkmated after 4 Ke2 Qxe4++.

4 ... Qxe4+

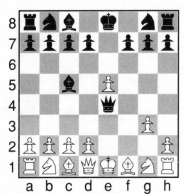

Diagram 144. Position after 4 ... Qxe4+.

Black forks the White King and Rook. After *5 Qe2*, Black can win the Rook with *5 ... Qxh1*.

The next example is from the "King's Gambit *Accepted*." Black will accept the White Pawn sacrifice.

1 e4 e5 2 f4 exf4

Black is now threatening 3 ... Qh4+.

3 Nf3

White develops the Knight and guards the h4 square.

3 ... g5 4 Bc4 f6??

This opens up the "h5–e8" diagonal leading directly to the King. See if you can find the winning move for White in Diagram 145.

Diagram 145. *Position after 4 . . . f6??—White has a winning sacrifice.*

White sacrifices a Knight, opening up the "d1–h5" diagonal for the Queen.

5 Nxg5!

White is also threatening to fork the Black Queen and Rook with 6 Nf7.

5 . . . fxg5 6 Qh5+ Ke7

Diagram 146. *Position after 6 . . . Ke7—White can checkmate Black in three moves.*

From Diagram 146 White has a choice of two ways to checkmate Black in only three moves. Either

A. *7 Qf7+ Kd6 8 Qd5+ Ke7 9 Qe5++*

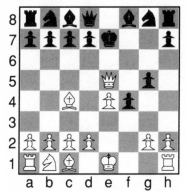

Diagram 147. Position after 9 Qe5++.

or

B. *7 Qxg5+ Ke8*

Black would also be checkmated after 7 ... Nf6 8
Qe5++, or 7 ... Kd6 8 Qd5+ Ke7 9 Qe5++.

8 Qh5+ Ke7 9 Qe5++ reaching the position in Diagram 148.

Diagram 148. Position after 9 Qe5++.

THE SKEWER OR X-RAY ATTACK

The "skewer," also known as the "X-ray attack," is another way you can win material. It is less common than the pin or fork. The skewer is used more often in the endgame and middlegame than in the opening.

The skewer is the opposite of a pin. A skewer is when a piece attacks an enemy piece that must move to avoid capture. When the enemy piece moves, it exposes another piece to attack. As in the pin, the piece that is attacked is lined up with another piece along a rank, a file, or a diagonal.

Let's take a look at an example of a skewer.

Diagram 149. White is skewering the Black King and Queen along the "d" file.

In Diagram 149 the White Rook has the Black King in check. After the King moves, White can play Rxd8 winning the Black Queen.

Another example of a skewer is shown in Diagram 150.

After the Black Queen moves out of attack, White can play Bxe8, capturing the Black Rook.

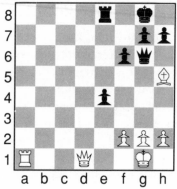

Diagram 150. *The Black Queen and Rook are being skewered on the "h5–e8" diagonal.*

See if you can find the skewer in Diagram 151, which is reached after the following moves:

1 e4 e5 2 Nc3 Bc5 3 Na4 Bxf2+ 4 Kxf2 Qh4+ 5 Kf3? d5! 6 d3??

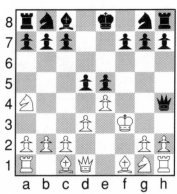

Diagram 151. *It is Black's move—can you find the skewer?*

Black can win the White Queen with *6 . . . Bg4+ 7 Ke3 Bxd1.*

Now that we have covered a lot of tactical motifs, it's time to cover the endgame in more detail.

THE KING
AND PAWN ENDGAME

Before you learn more complicated endgames you should study basic King and Pawn endings, because sometimes it only takes an extra Pawn to win a game! Usually, the main objective for the Pawn will be to reach the other side of the board and be promoted to a Queen. Often, though, the King must help the advance of his Pawn.

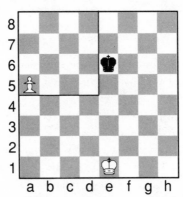

Diagram 152. If the enemy King gets within the square, it can catch the Pawn.

There is a simple way of figuring out whether or not an enemy King can catch a Pawn before it can successfully Queen. It is called "the rule of the square."

Draw a square around the Pawn, like the one in Diagram 152. If the enemy King is within the square of the Pawn or enters it on that move, the King can capture it in time.

Don't forget: If the Pawn is on the second rank, it can move two squares forward! If this is the case, then you need to draw the square as if the Pawn were on the third rank (instead of the second).

In Diagram 153 the White King is attacking all of the squares in front of the Pawn.

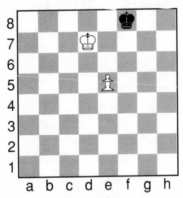

Diagram 153. The White King supports the advance of the Pawn.

Black is defenseless against the advance of the White Pawn. White will win by playing *1 e6*, followed by *2 e7* and *3 e8 = Q*.

The position in Diagram 153 was reached from the position in Diagram 154.

The extra Pawn will always win if the Pawn is on the fifth rank and the King is on the square directly in front of the Pawn (on the sixth rank). This is called the "basic winning position." The one exception is if the Pawn is on the "a" or "h" file (I'll talk about this later).

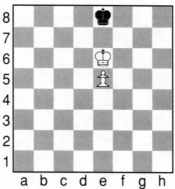

Diagram 154. The basic winning position.

When the basic winning position is achieved, it does not matter whose turn it is to move—the extra pawn *always* wins (if you play correctly of course!). Below is an example of how White will win from Diagram 154 if it is Black's turn to move.

1 . . . Kd8

Or, if 1 . . . Kf8, then White plays 2 Kd7, reaching the position in Diagram 153.

2 Kf7

The King will support his Pawn's advance. If White plays 2 Kd6, then Black plays 2 . . . Ke8. If White then tries to advance his Pawn with 3 e6 Kd8 4 e7+, then after 4 . . . Ke8 the position in Diagram 155 is reached.

This is a situation called "Zugzwang" (pronounced "tsoog-tsvong," a German word meaning "requirement to move"). This is when the player whose turn it is would rather not make a move because there are no good moves! In Diagram 155 any move that White makes either loses his Pawn or allows stalemate, resulting in a draw. If White plays 5 Ke6 to keep the Pawn defended, then Black is stalemated! Now back to the moves after 2 Kf7.

129

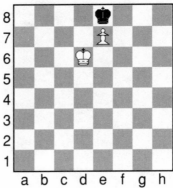

Diagram 155. White's move—White is in "Zugzwang."

2 ... Kd7 3 e6+ Kd8 4 e7+ Kd7 5 e8=Q+

White has Queened the Pawn and should soon checkmate Black.

Now let's go back to Diagram 154 and take a look at how the extra Pawn will win if it's White's turn to move.

1 Kd6

White can also win in a similar way after 1 Kf6 Kf8 2 e6 Ke8 3 e7 Kd7 4 Kf7 followed by 5 e8=Q.

1 ... Kd8 2 e6 Ke8 3 e7

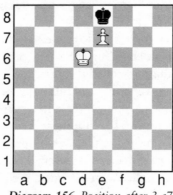

Diagram 156. Position after 3 e7.

130

Now Black is in Zugzwang! Black would like to keep the King in front of the White Pawn. However, the King must move.

3 . . . Kf7 4 Kd7

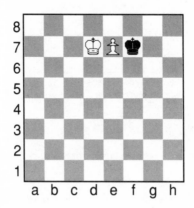

Diagram 157. Position after 4 Kd7.

White first covers the e8 square with the King before advancing the Pawn. Black cannot stop White from Queening the Pawn. Next move White will play *5 e8 = Q.*

A King on the sixth rank in front of the Pawn on the fifth rank results in a draw if:

1. the Pawn is an "a" or "h" Pawn, *and*
2. the enemy King can get in front of the Pawn.

The enemy King can't be driven out of the corner in front of the Pawn.

White's attempt to win with the "a" Pawn is hopeless. Let's take a look at how the game could continue from Diagram 158 if it's White's move.

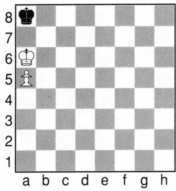

Diagram 158. The "a" Pawn is only good enough for a draw.

***1 Kb6 Kb8 2 a6 Ka8 3 a7**: stalemate.*

If it's Black's move, an attempt to win is equally hopeless.

1 . . . Kb8 2 Kb6 Ka8 3 a6 Kb8 4 a7+ Ka8

White is now in Zugzwang. White must either move away from the Pawn and lose it, or play *5 Ka6*—stalemate.

The position in Diagram 159 is also a draw, with Black to move.

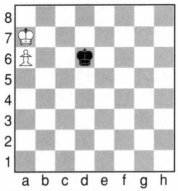

Diagram 159. Black to move—a draw.

Black can *force* the White King to stay in front of his own Pawn with

1 . . . Kc7 2 Ka8 Kc8 3 a7 Kc7: stalemate.

White has stalemated *himself!*

THE MAIN LINE OF THE RUY LOPEZ

The moves up to White's fifth move were covered in Lesson Nine. I recommend the Main Line of the Ruy Lopez for both White and Black. Let's pick up where we left off in Lesson Nine.

1 e4 e5 2 Nf3 Nc6 3 Bb5 a6 4 Ba4 Nf6 5 0–0 Be7

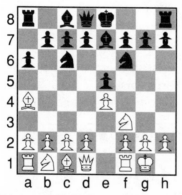

Diagram 160. Position after 5 . . . Be7.

Black develops his Bishop while shielding the King along the "e" file. This is a better move for Black than 5 . . . Nxe4 (the Open Variation I talked about in the last lesson). Now that the Black King is shielded against a Rook attack along the "e" file, Black threatens to play 6 . . . Nxe4.

6 Re1

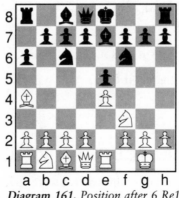

Diagram 161. Position after 6 Re1.

White defends the "e" Pawn and brings the Rook to a more active post. Defending the "e" Pawn with either 6 Nc3 or 6 d3 are okay moves, but White has a more active plan. White plans to attack boldly in the center with the "d" Pawn. In order to support the advance of the Pawn to d4, White will first move a Pawn to c3.

6 ... b5

This drives the White Bishop off the "a4–e8" diagonal and prevents White from playing 7 Bxc6. The natural-looking 6 ... 0–0 would lose a Pawn after 7 Bxc6 dxc6 8 Nxe5.

7 Bb3

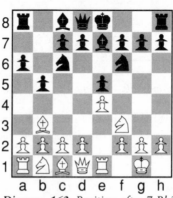

Diagram 162. Position after 7 Bb3.

White saves the Bishop from attack and puts it on the long "a2–g8" diagonal.

7 . . . d6

This opens up the "c8–h3" diagonal for the Bishop and defends the "e" Pawn a second time. The Black Knight is now free to go to a5 and attack the White Bishop.

8 c3

White opens up c2 for possible use by the Bishop and prepares to support the advance of the "d" Pawn to d4. Playing an immediate 8 d4 may lead to the "Noah's Ark Trap" (which I'll talk about in the next lesson).

8 . . . 0–0

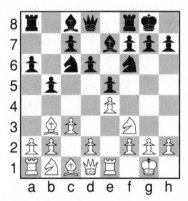

Diagram 163. Position after 8 . . . 0–0.

Black gets the King into safety and will have a more active Rook.

9 h3

This move prevents a possible pin by the Black Bishop. If White immediately attacks in the center with 9 d4, then Black has a strong pin with 9 . . . Bg4.

9 . . . Na5

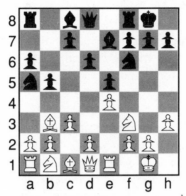

Diagram 164. *Position after 9 . . . Na5.*

The Black Knight goes to the edge of the board. This usually isn't a good idea. However, Black has two good reasons for moving the Knight to a5:

1. The Knight attacks the active White Bishop and will drive it off the long "a2–g8" diagonal.
2. Black can now expand on the Queenside by advancing the "c" Pawn.

10 Bc2

White doesn't want to allow Black to play 10 . . . Nxb3, trading off the Knight for the good Bishop. So White saves the Bishop for future use!

10 . . . c5

Black expands on the Queenside, opening up the "a5–d8" diagonal for the Queen and putting another attacker on the "d4" square.

11 d4

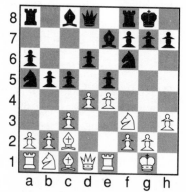

Diagram 165. Position after 11 d4.

White boldly attacks in the center with a Pawn. White is attacking the Black "e" Pawn with two pieces, while it is only defended by one piece.

11 ... Qc7

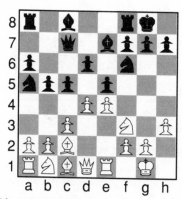

Diagram 166. Position after 11 ... Qc7.

Black brings the Queen to a safe but active post, where it helps defend the "e" Pawn. If White were to play 12 dxe5, then after 12 . . . dxe5, White wouldn't want to play 13 Nxe5?? because Black would capture a Knight with 13 . . . Qxe5.

Another good move for Black to defend the "e" Pawn is 11 . . . Nd7. This is known as the "Keres Variation" of the Ruy Lopez.

After 11 . . . Qc7 part of White's plan is to develop the Queenside Knight with 12 Nbd2. The Knight can then go to f1 with the idea of coming out toward the center by going to e3.

Here is an example of how the game might continue from Diagram 166:

12 Nbd2 Bd7 13 Nf1 Rfe8 14 b3 cxd4 15 cxd4 Rac8 16 Ne3 g6 17 Bb2 Bf8 18 Rc1 Qb8

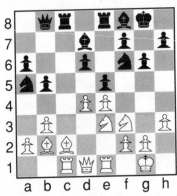

Diagram 167. Position after 18 . . . Qb8.

The above position was reached between the author and John Grefe (the former United States Champion) in 1973. It ended in a draw on the thirty-sixth move. Some people analyze very complex openings through the thirtieth move! Beginners usually don't study the openings beyond the first ten or twelve moves, though. But as you play more games, these openings will become more familiar and you'll be able to go farther.

13

░░░░░░░░░░░░░░░░░░░░░░

MORE TACTICAL MOTIFS

It's time to expand your knowledge of tactical motifs from Lesson Eleven.

THE NOAH'S ARK TRAP

One of the most famous traps used in the Ruy Lopez opening is the Noah's Ark Trap. One student asked me why it's called that. I told him that it is *very* old, like Noah's Ark.

In the Noah's Ark Trap White plays the first seven moves in the Main Line of the Ruy Lopez (I first discussed it in Lesson Nine, but went further in Lesson Twelve). Let's take a look at the moves leading up to the Noah's Ark Trap.

1 e4 e5 2 Nf3 Nc6 3 Bb5 a6 4 Ba4 Nf6 5 0–0 Be7 6 Re1 b5 7 Bb3 d6 8 d4?

White makes the mistake of attacking in the center too early with the "d" Pawn. White should play 8 c3 in order to support the Pawn first.

It's difficult for a beginner to think far enough ahead to find all of the moves. So as to make it easier, let's look at

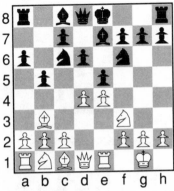

Diagram 168. Position after 8 d4?.

the position just before the end of the trap—that way you'll
know what kind of position you are striving for. See if you
can find the move in Diagram 169 for Black that will win
the White Bishop in two moves.

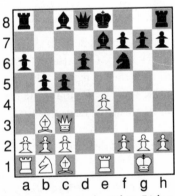

Diagram 169. Black can win the White Bishop in two moves.

After **11 . . . c4** the White Bishop is trapped and will be
captured on the next move. Now, go back to the position
in Diagram 168 and try to find the moves that lead to the
position in Diagram 169.

Let's look at the moves after 8 d4 (from Diagram 168).

8 ... exd4

This captures a Pawn, and Black will use the Pawn on d4 as bait for the rest of the trap.

9 Nxd4??

This leads to the loss of a minor piece—it's better not to capture the Pawn.

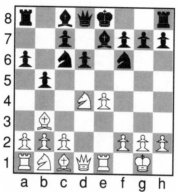

Diagram 170. Position after 9 Nxd4??

9 ... Nxd4

Black will force White to bring the Queen out to recapture the Knight. The Queen will then be used as a target to gain time for the advance of the Black "c" Pawn.

10 Qxd4

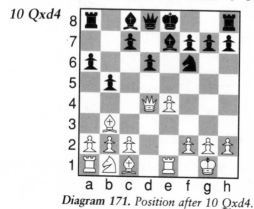

Diagram 171. Position after 10 Qxd4.

10 . . . c5 11 Qc3

This reaches the position in Diagram 169. White must lose the Bishop after 11 . . . c4. It would be best for White to get two Pawns in exchange for the Bishop with 12 Bxc4 bxc4 13 Qxc4.

"A KNIGHT ON THE RIM IS DIM"

We have already learned that "a Knight on the rim is dim." On the edge of the board it can move to fewer squares than when it's in the center. Here's an example of how to take advantage of a Knight on the edge of the board.

The position in Diagram 172 is reached after the following moves.

1 e4 e5 2 Nf3 Nc6 3 Bc4 Bc5 4 c3 Nf6 5 d4 exd4 6 cxd4 Bb6? 7 d5 Na5 8 Bd3 d6??

See if you can find the move that will win a Black Knight in two moves.

Diagram 172. White can win a Knight in two moves.

White should play **9 b4!**. The Knight on a5 is under attack by the Pawn and cannot move anywhere without getting captured.

THE DISCOVERED ATTACK AND DISCOVERED CHECK

A "discovered attack" happens when a piece moves and gets out of the way of another piece (of the same color) that attacks an enemy piece. (It's called "discovered" because your opponent *discovers* what you're doing when you dis-cover the attacking piece!) Often two threats can be created at the same time. The discovered attack is a dangerous weapon. A discovered attack can be tricky, and is often discovered by the opponent too late!

In Diagram 173 White can use a discovered attack to win a Pawn. The White Queen can't capture the Knight on h5 because the White Knight on f3 is in the way. Moving that Knight opens up the "d1–h5" diagonal for use by the White Queen. See if you can find White's move.

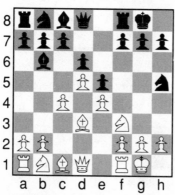

Diagram 173. White can win a Pawn in two moves.

White can win a Pawn with *1 Nxe5 dxe5 2 Qxh5*. This is an example of how you can take advantage of an enemy Knight on the edge of the board.

Black can win a Pawn in Diagram 174 through the use of a discovered attack. See if you can find Black's key move.

The key move is *1 . . . Nxd5!*. This uncovers the Black

143

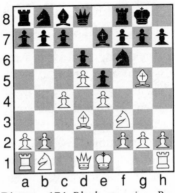

Diagram 174. Black can win a Pawn.

Bishop with an attack on the White Bishop on g5. Even though the "d" Pawn is well defended, it's lost. If White captures the Black Knight with either *2 cxd5* or *2 exd5*, then Black recovers the piece with *2 ... Bxg5*. Also, if White trades off Bishops with *2 Bxe7*, Black saves the Knight and recaptures the Bishop with *2 ... Nxe7*. This type of discovered attack is often overlooked even by experienced players.

In Diagram 175 White can win the Black Queen in two moves, using a discovered attack. See if you can find the moves.

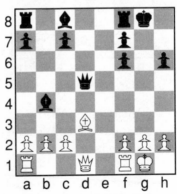

Diagram 175. White can win the Black Queen in two moves.

The winning move is *1 Bh7+*. This opens up the "d" file for the White Queen, exposing the Black undefended Queen to attack. *And* the Black King is in check! After Black gets the King out of check with *1 ... Kxh7*, White captures the Black Queen with *2 Qxd5*.

The position in Diagram 176 is reached from an opening known as the "French Defense." White can win the Black Queen by using a discovered attack. After making the moves leading up to the position in Diagram 176, see if you can find White's winning moves.

1 e4 e6 2 d4 d5 3 e5 c5 4 c3 Nc6 5 Nf3 Qb6 6 Bd3 cxd4 7 cxd4 Nxd4?? 8 Nxd4 Qxd4??

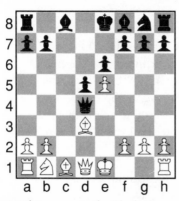

Diagram 176. White can win the Black Queen in two moves.

White plays *9 Bb5+* with a discovered attack on the Black Queen. After *9 ... Bd7 10 Bxd7+ Kxd7 11 Qxd4* the Black Queen is no more!

A "discovered check" is much like a discovered attack, except that the uncovered piece (the attacking piece that hasn't moved) attacks the King. The discovered check is often deadly.

In Diagram 177 White can use a discovered check to win the Black Queen. See if you can find the move.

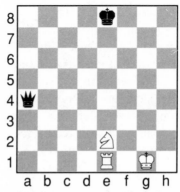

Diagram 177. White can capture the Black Queen in two moves.

The winning move is *1 Nc3+*. The Black King is in check by the Rook, while the Black Queen is under attack by the Knight. After the Black King gets out of check, White can capture the Black Queen.

A famous trap using the discovered check comes out of an opening known as "Petroff's Defense." Have you ever had an opponent make the same moves as you? Here is a good example of how to take advantage of someone who tries to copy you. You can "beat him at his own game!"

1 e4 e5 2 Nf3 Nf6

This move is the beginning of the Petroff's Defense. Black answers White's attack on the Black "e" Pawn with a counterattack on White's "e" Pawn.

3 Nxe5

It's good simply to capture the Pawn. Another good move for White is to attack boldly in the center with 3 d4.

3 . . . Nxe4?

This is going to get Black into trouble. It's better for Black to play 3 . . . d6 4 Nf3 Nxe4. At that point White can get a foothold in the center and free the Queenside pieces with *5 d4*.

4 Qe2!

The Queen attacks the undefended Black Knight and is lined up with the Black King. If Black continues to copy White with 4 . . . Qe7 then White captures the Black Knight with 5 Qxe4.

4 . . . Nf6??

This allows White to capture the Black Queen with a discovered check. See if you can find it in Diagram 178.

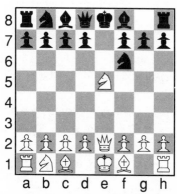

Diagram 178. Position after 4 . . . Nf6??.

White plays *5 Nc6 +*. After Black gets the King out of check, White can capture the Queen with the Knight.

Some beginners have tried playing 5 Nxf7 +. However, Black can get out of check *and* win the Knight after 5 . . . Kxf7.

A "double check" is a type of discovered check, except that *both* the uncovered piece *and* the piece that moves attack the King. The *only* way to get out of a double check is to move the King.

In Diagram 179 White uses a double check to force a quick checkmate. See if you can find White's best move.

White begins with *1 Bg5 +*. The Black King is in check

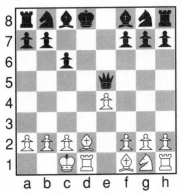

Diagram 179. White can checkmate Black in two moves.

by both the Rook and Bishop. 1 Ba5 + is also a double check. However, Black would not be checkmated on the next move.

After 1 Bg5 + Black has a choice of being checkmated after *1 . . . Ke8 2 Rd8 + +* or *1 . . . Kc7 2 Bd8 + +*.

THE OVERWORKED DEFENDER

An overworked defender is a piece that is defending too many pieces or important squares at the same time. You

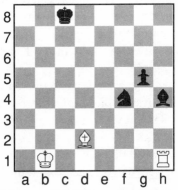

Diagram 180. White can win a piece.

can take advantage of an overworked defender because it can't be in two places at the same time!

In Diagram 180 the Pawn is defending both the Knight and the Bishop.

White can take advantage of the overworked Pawn by playing *1 Bxf4 gxf4 2 Rxh4.*

In Diagram 181 White can win the Black Queen in two moves by taking advantage of an overworked King. The King is defending both the Queen and the "f" Pawn. If White plays 1 Qxd8 +, Black can recapture the Queen with 1 . . . Kxd8. Can you find the White move that wins the Queen?

Diagram 181. White can win the Black Queen in two moves.

White forces the Black King to move away from the defense of the Queen with *1 Bxf7 + !.* Black has no choice but to capture the Bishop with *1 . . . Kxf7*, allowing *2 Qxd8.*

In Diagram 182 the Black Queen on b8 is defending the Rook on b2 *and* preventing White from using a backrank mate with 1 Re8. But the Queen can't be in two places at the same time! Find White's winning move.

White wins the Rook with *1 Qxb2!.* Black is unable to

capture the White Queen with *1 . . . Qxb2??* because of the backrank mate *2 Re8+ +*.

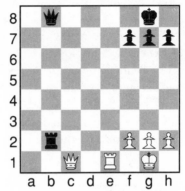

Diagram 182. White can capture a Rook.

MORE ON THE KING AND PAWN VERSUS KING ENDGAME

In the last lesson we started looking at the basic endgame of King and Pawn against a King. Now I'll show you more about this type of endgame.

In Diagram 183, with correct play it is a draw if it's White's turn to move. If it is Black's turn to move, the game will end in a win for White (with correct play).

Another important idea is called the "opposition." This often happens in King and Pawn endings. An opposition exists where there is an odd number (one, three, or five) of squares between two Kings on a rank, file, or diagonal. The player whose turn it is to move must end up giving ground to the enemy King and is at a disadvantage. The player not having the turn to move is at an advantage and is said to "have the opposition." This is rather difficult to understand right away, so it may take you a while to get the hang of it. But be patient—you will!

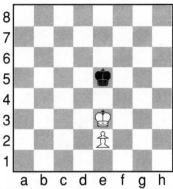

Diagram 183. If it's White's move, a draw—if it's Black's move, a win for White.

From the position in Diagram 183 we'll first take a look at how Black can draw if it is White's turn to move. Then we will take a look at how White can win if it's Black's turn to move. Remember that the basic winning position was covered in Lesson Twelve (see Diagram 154). You can go back and refresh your memory if necessary.

If it's White's move in Diagram 183, Black can draw by playing the right moves. Black will keep on opposing the White King and preventing it from moving farther in front of its Pawn. Black has "the opposition."

1 Kd3

If White plays 1 Kf3, then Black can oppose the White King with 1 . . . Kf5.

1 . . . Kd5

Black's last move opposes the White King, which prevents it from moving farther in front of the Pawn. White will try to support the advance of the Pawn by keeping the King in front of it.

151

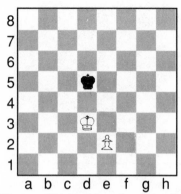

Diagram 184. Position after 1 . . . Kd5.

2 e4 +

White realizes that there is no way to make progress just by moving the King—so the Pawn advances. A general rule of thumb: Once the King falls behind its Pawn the game will end in a draw. The only exception to this may be after the basic winning position is reached.

2 . . . Ke5

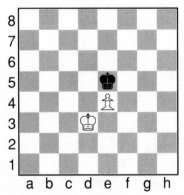

Diagram 185. Position after 2 . . . Ke5.

3 Ke3 Ke6

The Black King can oppose the White King on either side of the Pawn.

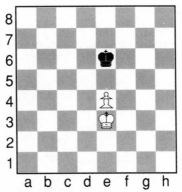

Diagram 186. *Position after 3 . . . Ke6.*

4 Kf4 Kf6 5 e5+ Ke6 6 Ke4 Ke7 7 Kd5 Kd7 8 e6+ Ke7 9 Ke5 Ke8 10 Kd6 Kd8 11 e7+

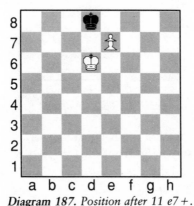

Diagram 187. *Position after 11 e7 +.*

Another rule of thumb: When the Pawn reaches the seventh rank, the game will result in a draw *if the Pawn is checking the King.* If the Black King were on e8 and not in check (after 11 e7), then White could have won.

11 . . . Ke8 12 Ke6: stalemate.

Now let's go back to Diagram 183 and look at how White can win if it is Black's move. The Black King must step to the side and give ground to the White King.

1 . . . Kd5

If Black plays 1 . . . Kf5, then White can move the King forward with 2 Kd4.

2 Kf4

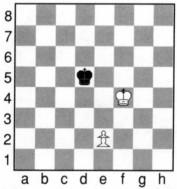

Diagram 188. *Position after 2 Kf4.*

It is important for the King to support the advance of the Pawn by staying in front of it. If your King is in front of the Pawn, and there is *at least one open square* between them, then (if you play well) you will always win. The exception is with an "a" or "h" Pawn (I talked about this in the last lesson).

2 ... Ke6 3 Ke4 Kf6 4 Kd5

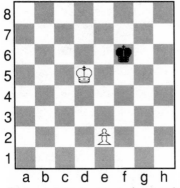

Diagram 189. Position after 4 Kd5.

4 ... Kf5

Black is trying to stop constantly losing ground. If Black kept on retreating, the game would continue with 4 ... Ke7 5 Ke5 Kd7 6 Kf6 Ke8 7 Ke6 Kd8 8 e4 Ke8 9 e5, reaching the basic winning position.

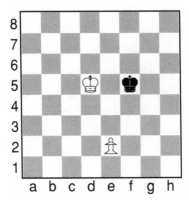

Diagram 190. Position after 4 ... Kf5.

5 e4+ Kf6 6 Kd6

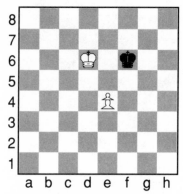

Diagram 191. *Position after 6 Kd6.*

White keeps the King out in front of the Pawn in order to support its advance.

6 . . . Kf7 7 e5 Ke8

See if you can find White's move that ends up in the basic winning position.

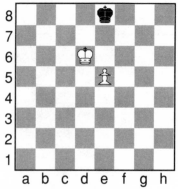

Diagram 192. *Position after 7 . . . Ke8.*

8 Ke6!

White is in the basic winning position (see Lesson Twelve, Diagram 154).

THE SICILIAN DEFENSE AND OTHER DEFENSES TO 1 e4

There are many moves against 1 e4 other than 1 . . . e5. The "Sicilian Defense" is one of the most common. It can lead to a *very* complicated game, so it's one of the most analyzed openings. It's recommended that you play 1 . . . e5 against 1 e4 when playing Black. We'll study the Sicilian Defense from White's point of view.

Let's take a look at this opening.

1 e4 c5

Diagram 193. *Position after 1 . . . c5.*

With 1 . . . c5 Black is using the Sicilian Defense. The "c" Pawn attacks the important d4 square. Black also releases the Queen on the "d8–a5" diagonal. In the Sicilian Defense, Black usually plays actively on the Queenside as well as in the center.

Let's take a brief look at other common replies to 1 e4.

THE FRENCH DEFENSE

This is another popular defense to 1 e4. Black plays 1 . . . e6 with the idea of supporting 2 . . . d5. If you aren't immediately challenged in the center after 1 e4 and you can place a second Pawn in the center with 2 d4, *then do it!* The Pawn on d4 gives you a strong Pawn center and releases the Bishop on the "c1–h6" diagonal.

After 1 e4 e6 2 d4, Black will usually challenge the center with 2 . . . d5 (attacking the undefended White Pawn on e4). White can defend the Pawn and develop a Knight with 3 Nc3. One of the problems of the French Defense is that the Black Bishop on c8 is difficult to develop. The game might continue: 3 . . . Nf6 (or 3 . . . Bb4 4 e5) 4 Bg5 Be7 5 e5 Nfd7 6 Bxe7 Qxe7 7 f4.

THE CARO-KANN DEFENSE

This isn't used as often as the French Defense. Against 1 e4 Black plays 1 . . . c6 (preparing to support an attack in the center with the "d" Pawn). Once again, if you can put a Pawn strongly in the center with 2 d4, *do it!* When Black attacks in the center with 2 . . . d5, you should defend your "e" Pawn with 3 Nc3. The game might continue: 3 . . . dxe4 4 Nxe4 Bf5 5 Ng3.

THE PIRC DEFENSE

This doesn't immediately challenge White in the center. After 1 e4 Black plays 1 . . . d6. Once again, 2 d4 is best. If Black attacks your "e" Pawn with 2 . . . Nf6, you should defend it with 3 Nc3. From there Black might play: 3 . . . g6 (Black plans to use a "fianchetto" development of the Bishop—I'll explain this later in this lesson) 4 g3 Bg7 5 Bg2 0–0 6 Nge2.

ALEKHINE'S DEFENSE

This immediately attacks your "e" Pawn after 1 e4 Nf6. You can get your "e" Pawn out of attack and attack the Black Knight with 2 e5. When Black moves the Knight with 2 . . . Nd5, White should bring a second Pawn into the center with 3 d4. The game might continue: 3 . . . d6 4 Bc4 Nb6 5 Bb3 dxe5 6 Qh5 e6 7 dxe5.

THE CENTER-COUNTER DEFENSE

This is used quite often by inexperienced players who haven't studied their openings very carefully. After 1 e4 Black immediately attacks in the center with 1 . . . d5. White's best move then is to capture the Pawn with 2 exd5, in order to draw the Black Queen out. (I explained this in Lesson Seven, when we looked at the game against the Dumb Computer.) If Black doesn't bring the Queen out early and plays 2 . . . Nf6 instead, then you should bring another Pawn into the center with 3 d4. The game might continue: 3 . . . Nxd5 4 c4 Nb6 5 Nf3.

Now let's return to our discussion of the Sicilian Defense.

2 f4

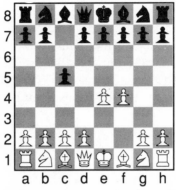

Diagram 194. Position after 2 f4.

This move helps White to build up a Pawn center and to get an active game on the Kingside. This isn't the most common move played here! Most masters play 2 Nf3, hoping to support an attack in the center with 3 d4. This is a *very* good idea. However, playing 3 d4 leads to a very complicated game. That's why I recommend 2 f4. You may even catch a *more* experienced player off guard with this *less* common move!

2 . . . Nc6 3 Nf3

Diagram 195. Position after 3 Nf3.

Both sides have developed Knights toward the center, challenging the important d4 and e5 squares.

3 ... d6

Black opens up the "c8–h3" diagonal for the Bishop while defending the "c" Pawn and attacking the e5 square.

4 Bb5

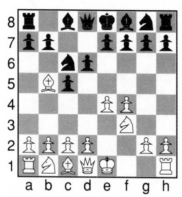

Diagram 196. Position after 4 Bb5.

The Bishop is actively developed and pins the Knight on c6. Black must be concerned about the possibility of White playing 5 Bxc6 +, which would give Black doubled Pawns after 5 ... bxc6. As mentioned before, doubled Pawns are usually a weakness.

4 ... Bd7

Black defends the Knight on c6 and plans to meet 5 Bxc6 with 5 ... Bxc6, avoiding doubled Pawns. The Bishop move also unpins the Knight.

5 Nc3

White continues to develop minor pieces toward the center.

5 . . . g6

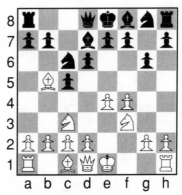

***Diagram 197.** Position after 5 . . . g6.*

Black plans to use a "fianchetto." A fianchetto is the flank (that is, from the side) development of a Bishop in the opening of the game. In order to fianchetto a Bishop, you usually move a "b" or "g" Pawn to clear the way for the Bishop. White would fianchetto a Bishop by placing it on either b2 or g2. Black would fianchetto a Bishop by placing it on either b7 or g7. The use of a fianchetto is common for Black in the Sicilian Defense.

"Fianchetto" is an Italian word. When I asked one student what it meant he said, "I think a fianchetto is a giant knife used to carve chess pieces from wood!" He must have been thinking of a stiletto!

6 0–0

White gets the King into safety. The Rook is also active on the "f" file because the "f" Pawn was moved.

6 . . . Bg7

Black completes the fianchetto of the Bishop.

7 d3

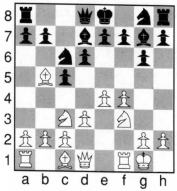

Diagram 198. Position after 7 d3.

White defends the Pawn on e4 again and opens up the "c1–h6" diagonal for the Bishop. White is ready to complete the development of the minor pieces by developing the Bishop at c1. Part of White's plan may be to build up on the Kingside by bringing the Queen into play with moves like Qe1 followed by Qh4. White has a comfortable position.

ADVANCED TACTICAL MOTIFS

Now it's time to look at some advanced tactical ideas. If you analyze your games (with the written records you keep in algebraic notation), soon you'll be able to plan your moves. If you work at it, you'll be able to think two to three moves ahead.

MORE ATTACKS ON WEAK f2 AND f7 SQUARES

Look at the following attacks against the weak f2 and f7 squares.

In Diagram 199 Black can win a Knight at the very least.

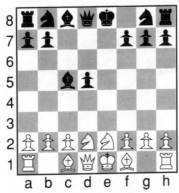

Diagram 199. Black to move and win at least a Knight.

Here's a hint: it involves an attack on White's "f" Pawn. See if you can find Black's move.

The best move for Black is *1 . . . Qb6!*, threatening to checkmate White on the next move with 2 . . . Bxf2 + +. If White plays 2 Nf3, then Black can checkmate in two moves with 2 . . . Bxf2+ 3 Kd2 Qe3 + +. After 1 . . . Qb6! the best White can do is to give up a Knight in order to prevent checkmate with 2 Nd4 Bxd4 3 Qf3.

The next position involves an attack on f7, a fork, and a discovered attack. See if you can find how White can win

Diagram 200. White to move and win material.

material in Diagram 200. You must think ahead three moves.

White begins with *1 Bxf7+*. After Black accepts White's Bishop sacrifice with *1 . . . Kxf7*, White plays *2 Nxe5+* with a discovered attack by the Queen on the Black Bishop, and a fork on the Black King and Bishop. If *2 . . . Ke8*, then White can bring the Queen actively into play with *3 Qxg4*, reaching the position in Diagram 201.

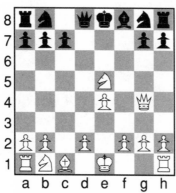

Diagram 201. Position after 3 Qxg4.

From Diagram 201 if Black attacks the White Queen with *3 . . . Nf6* then White has a forced win of the Black Rook on h8 in five moves! Here are some hints to help you out:

1. All of White's moves will put the King in check (except for the final move which captures the Rook with a Knight).
2. The fourth move is a Knight fork on f7, which will involve getting the Black King to d8 in a few moves.

Now, try to find the moves that win the Black Rook in five moves from Diagram 202.

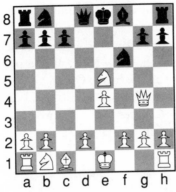

Diagram 202. White to move and win a Rook in five moves!

Here are the winning moves: **4 Qe6+ Qe7** (not 4 ...
Be7??, because of 5 Qf7++) **5 Qc8+ Qd8 6 Qxd8+
Kxd8 7 Nf7+**, followed by **8 Nxh8**.

In Diagram 203 White can win a minor piece. See if you
can find the key move for White.

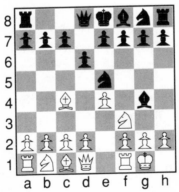

Diagram 203. White to move and win at least a minor piece.

The pin on the White Knight isn't very effective. White plays *1 Nxe5!*, winning the Knight. If Black tries to win the White Queen with *1 . . . Bxd1??*, then Black is checkmated with *2 Bxf7 + +*. Therefore, after 1 Nxe5!, Black has nothing better than 1 . . . dxe5, allowing 2 Qxg4.

One of the most famous Queen sacrifices is known as "Legal's Mate." The idea is similar to the last position. Let's look at the moves.

1 e4 e5 2 Nf3 d6 3 Bc4 Bg4 4 Nc3 g6?

White can win at least a Pawn with the brilliant offer of a Queen sacrifice. Can you find the best move for White in Diagram 204?

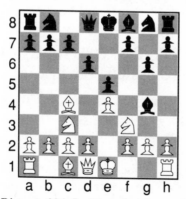

Diagram 204. Position after 4 . . . g6?.

White plays *5 Nxe5!*. If Black is greedy and takes the White Queen with *5 . . . Bxd1??*, White has a quick checkmate. See if you can find the checkmate in two moves for White in Diagram 205.

*Diagram 205. Position after 5 . . . Bxd1??—White can checkmate
Black in two moves.*

White forces a checkmate with **6 Bxf7+ Ke7 7
Nd5 + +**. It would certainly have been better for Black to
refuse the Queen sacrifice and lose a Pawn with 5 . . . dxe5
6 Qxg4.

SOME BRILLIANT QUEEN SACRIFICES
TO FORCE CHECKMATE

A queen sacrifice to force checkmate is certainly one of the
most satisfying ways to win a game. Here are a couple of
famous positions where brilliant Queen sacrifices were
made.

In Diagram 206 White forced checkmate in two moves,
beginning with a Queen sacrifice. See if you can find it.

White forced a quick checkmate with **1 Qxf7+! Rxf7
2 Re8 + +**. The Rook on f7 is pinned by the Bishop on b3.
Even if Black refuses the White Queen with 1 . . . Kh8, it is
still checkmate by 2 Qxf8 + +.

One of the most famous checkmates is known as Philidor's Legacy. It involves a series of moves using a Queen
sacrifice to force a smothered mate (which I explained in

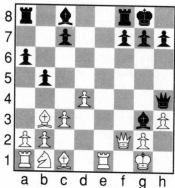

Diagram 206. White can checkmate in two moves.

Lesson Ten). I discussed the final move leading to Phili-dor's Legacy in Lesson Ten (see Diagram 122). If you re-view the position in Diagram 122, it will help you know what you want to accomplish in Diagram 207.

In Diagram 207 White can force a checkmate in two moves by using Philidor's Legacy. See if you can find the moves.

Diagram 207. White to move and checkmate Black in two moves.

White forces checkmate with *1 Qg8 + ! Rxg8 2 Nf7 + +*.

Now that you've seen the solution to this position, can you find a checkmate in five moves in Diagram 208? The moves lead right into the same position as in Diagram 207. Another hint: Every move will put the Black King in check.

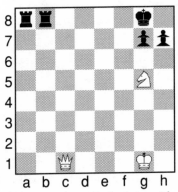

Diagram 208. White to move and checkmate Black in five moves.

White forces checkmate with *1 Qc4 + Kg8* (if 1 ... Kf8? then 2 Qf7 + +) *2 Nf7 + Kg8 3 Nh6 + Kh8* (if 3 ... Kf8? then 4 Qf7 + +) *4 Qg8 + ! Rxg8 5 Nf7 + +*.

So far, I haven't said much about Rooks, except for the "Rook Roller" in Lesson Eight. But now that you've learned more advanced tactics, we can move on to how to use Rooks.

THE USE OF ROOKS

Some special strategies apply to the use of Rooks during the game. Let's look at some of them more closely.

In Lesson Six, I noted that Rooks are not usually used actively in the opening. A few times, though, you've seen positions that use a Rook on an open file (a file that doesn't have a Pawn on it). A Rook can often get into play or be used to attack from a distance on an open file. As a rule of thumb: place Rooks on open files.

In Diagram 209 the White Rook on e1 is on an open file.

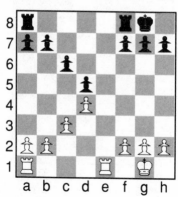

Diagram 206. *The White Rook on e1 is on an open file.*

When two Rooks of the same color are placed on an open file it is called "doubling Rooks." This can be very strong, because the Rooks support one another on the file. Rooks can also be doubled along a rank, as in Diagram 210.

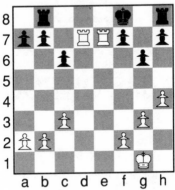

Diagram 210. The White Rooks are doubled on the seventh rank.

The seventh rank can be a strong place to double your Rooks. In Diagram 210 White's doubled Rooks will force the capture of material by attacking the Black Pawns. Even

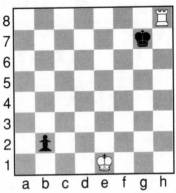

Diagram 211. Find White's move that will stop the Black Pawn from Queening.

172

placing one Rook on the seventh rank can be a very strong offensive move.

Rooks are very effective in the endgame because they can help stop enemy Pawns from advancing and being promoted to Queens. Placing a Rook behind an advancing enemy Pawn may stop it dead in its tracks! Can you find the move in Diagram 211 that prevents the Black Pawn from Queening?

White simply plays *1 Rb8* and the Rook will be able to capture the Black Pawn on the next move.

On the other hand, placing a Rook behind one of your own Pawns can help defend it and support its advance. In Diagram 212 the White Rook defends and supports the Pawn.

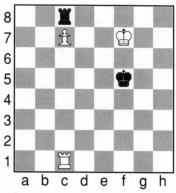

Diagram 212. The White Rook supports the Pawn from behind.

The Black Rook can't move without allowing the White Pawn to advance to c8 and become a Queen. Black won't be able to stop the White King from driving away the Rook after *1 Ke7*, followed by *2 Kd7*. Black will eventually have to give up the Rook in order to prevent White from getting a Queen.

CHECKMATE WITH A KING AND A ROOK VERSUS A LONE KING

It's important to know how to force checkmate with just a King and Rook against a lone King. You'll need to use your King actively along with the Rook in order to force the enemy King to the edge of the board. The position with a checkmate in one move is shown in Diagram 213.

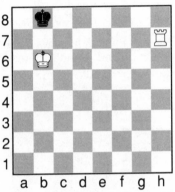

Diagram 213. White to move and checkmate Black in one move.

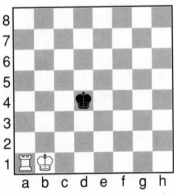

Diagram 214. White can force checkmate with the King and the Rook.

174

White checkmates Black with *1 Rh8 + +*. You can drive the enemy King to the edge of the board by using a simple pattern. You need to position your King across from the enemy King on a rank or file. Then your Rook checks the enemy King and drives it a rank or file closer to the edge of the board. It's best to look at an example of this, using Diagram 214 as a starting position.

1 Kc2

White begins to bring the King toward the Black King in the center.

1 . . . Ke4 2 Kc3 Kd5 3 Ra4

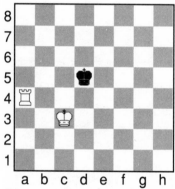

Diagram 215. *Position after 3 Ra4.*

White brings the Rook into play. The Black King now is limited to half the squares on the board. As the Rook moves up one rank at a time, the Black King will have fewer and fewer squares available.

3 . . . Ke5

Black tries to keep the King in the center. The White King will be lined up with the Black King before the Rook drives it back.

4 Kd3 Kd5

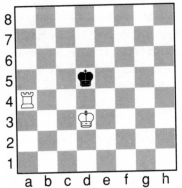

Diagram 216. Position after 4 . . . Kd5.

5 Ra5 + Kd6

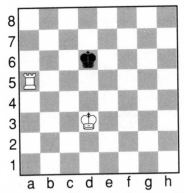

Diagram 217. Position after 5 . . . Kd6.

6 Ke4!

White wants to have the move once the Kings are lined up, so White doesn't immediately move the King directly across from the Black King. If White plays 6 Kd4 then the Black King can step aside with 6 ... Ke6, planning to meet 7 Ra6+ with 7 ... Kf5. In that case, White makes no progress. After 6 Kd4 Ke6, White does best to play 7 Rh5!, planning to meet 7 ... Kd6 with 8 Rh6+. White would lose time, but would be back on track.

6 ... Ke6 7 Ra6+ Kd7 8 Ke5 Ke7

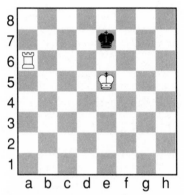

Diagram 218. *Position after 8 ... Ke7.*

If Black plays 8 ... Kc7 the game can continue 9 Kd5 Kb7 10 Rc6, and the Black King is limited to only four squares. The idea is to reduce the squares available to the enemy King.

9 Ra7+ Kd8 10 Ke6 Kc8

Not 10 ... Ke8 because of 11 Ra8++.

11 Kd6 Kb8 12 Rc7!

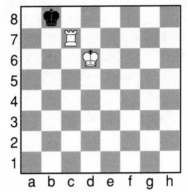

Diagram 219. Position after 12 Rc7!.

The Black King is limited to just two squares. White will now move the King in for the final kill!

12 . . . Ka8 13 Kc6 Kb8 14 Kb6 Ka8 15 Rc8 + +

Black has been checkmated. White certainly wouldn't want to play 15 Rb7?? That would be a stalemate!

It's now time for us to learn how to play against "d" Pawn openings as Black.

16

▝▝▝▝▝▝▝▝▝▝▝▝▝

QUEEN-PAWN OPENINGS

So far we've looked at openings beginning with 1 e4 (known as "King-Pawn openings"). When you play Black you should have a defense against White playing 1 d4 (known as "Queen-Pawn openings"). As White it's recommended that you play 1 e4 as an opening system. But if you're Black playing against White's 1 d4, you can develop an excellent system using the "Nimzo-Indian" or "Queen's Indian" defense.

THE NIMZO-INDIAN DEFENSE

The Nimzo-Indian Defense is a very active defense for Black. Many other defenses against 1 d4 give Black a cramped game, with little room to move the pieces.

1 d4

This is the second most popular opening move for White. It puts a Pawn in the center and opens up the "c1–h6" diagonal for the Bishop on c1.

1 . . . Nf6

Diagram 220. Position after 1 . . . Nf6.

Black develops a Knight toward the center and can attack the e4 square. This prevents White from getting a strong Pawn center with 2 e4. Another popular move for Black is 1 . . . d5.

2 c4

This is the most common second move for White. White uses a second Pawn to attack the center and opens up the "d1–a4" diagonal for the Queen. In Queen-Pawn openings both sides usually *don't* want to move their Knights in front of the "c" Pawn. White's position in the center and Queenside would have been cramped if 2 Nc3 had been played.

2 . . . e6

Black opens up the "f8–a3" diagonal for the Bishop on f8. The Pawn on e6 will be able to support the advance of the Black "d" Pawn to d5 later on.

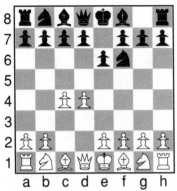

Diagram 221. Position after 2 . . . e6.

3 Nc3

White develops the Knight toward the center and threatens to get a strong Pawn center with 4 e4. Another common move for White here is 3 Nf3. I'll talk about this later, when we get to the Queen's Indian Defense.

3 . . . Bb4

Diagram 222. Position after 3 . . . Bb4.

Black develops the Bishop and pins the White Knight on c3. This prevents White from getting a strong Pawn center with 4 e4, because of 4 . . . Nxe4. Black has also cleared the way for Kingside castling.

4 e3

White defends the "d" Pawn again while opening up the "f1–a6" diagonal for the Bishop on f1. This fourth move leads to the "Rubinstein Variation," which is very popular for White.

4 . . . 0–0

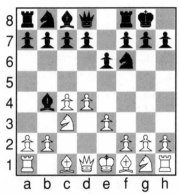

Diagram 223. Position after 4 . . . 0–0.

Black gets his King out of the center and into safety.

5 Bd3

White develops the Bishop by locating it on the long "b1–h7" diagonal.

5 . . . d5

Black finally uses a Pawn to attack in the center! This also helps to free Black's Queenside pieces.

Diagram 224. Position after 5 . . . d5.

6 Nf3

White develops a Knight toward the center and clears the way for the King to castle.

6 . . . c5

Black uses a second Pawn to attack in the center. Black would get a cramped game with 6 . . . Nc6. As mentioned before, it usually isn't good to develop a Knight in front of the "c" Pawn in a Queen-Pawn opening.

7 0–0 Nc6

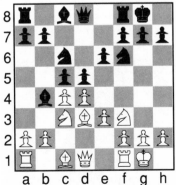

Diagram 225. Position after 7 . . . Nc6.

183

Black develops the other Knight toward the center. Both sides have three out of four minor pieces developed, their Kings are castled, and they have good Pawn centers. Here is an example of how the game might continue.

8 a3 Bxc3 9 bxc3 dxc4 10 Bxc4 Qc7

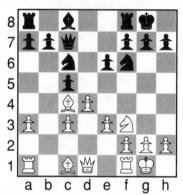

Diagram 226. Position after 10 . . . Qc7.

Black plans to play 11 . . . e5, attacking in the center and opening up the "c8–h3" diagonal for the Bishop on c8. White cannot win a Pawn with 11 dxc5 because of 11 . . . Na5 attacking the Bishop on c4 with the Knight and attacking the Pawn on c5 with the Queen.

THE QUEEN'S INDIAN DEFENSE

The first two moves for both sides are exactly the same as in the Nimzo-Indian Defense.

1 d4 Nf6 2 c4 e6 3 Nf3

White develops a Knight toward the center. But White is not immediately threatening 4 e4, so Black has time to use a Queenside fianchetto.

184

Diagram 227. Position after 3 Nf3.

Another possible move for White is 3 g3. This is known as the "Catalan Opening," in which White plans to fianchetto the Bishop to g2. Black would then do best to immediately attack in the center with 3 . . . d5.

3 . . . b6

Black is preparing to use a fianchetto. With the Bishop on b7 Black will attack the important e4 square a second time. This will help to prevent White from placing a Pawn on e4 and getting a strong Pawn center.

4 g3

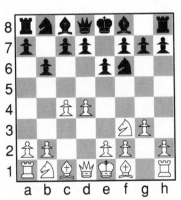

Diagram 228. Position after 4 g3.

White also prepares to fianchetto a Bishop. This will counter Black's fianchettoed bishop along the "h1–a8" diagonal. White could have also played *4 e3,* opening up the "f1–a6" diagonal for the Bishop. One possible way to play this after 4 e3 is 4 . . . Bb7 5 Bd3 d5 6 0–0 Bd6 7 Nc3 0–0 8 b3 Nbd7.

4 . . . Bb7 5 Bg2

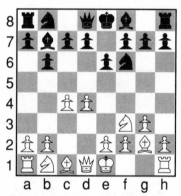

Diagram 229. *Position after 5 Bg2.*

Both sides have fianchettoed a Bishop.

5 . . . Be7

This is the best square for the other Bishop. Black is also clearing the way for castling. 5 . . . Bd6 is not good because it blocks the "d" Pawn. In the opening it usually isn't good to place a minor piece directly in front of an unmoved "d" or "e" Pawn. Most of the time it cramps your position. 5 . . . Bb4+ allows White to develop and challenge Black's Bishop with 6 Bd2.

6 0–0 0–0 7 Nc3

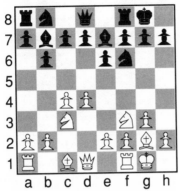

Diagram 230. Position after 7 Nc3.

White develops a Knight and attacks the important e4 square. Part of White's plan is to move the Queen to c2 in order to support moving a Pawn to e4.

7 ... Ne4

An important move for Black. Black occupies the important e4 square, setting up a temporary blockade. Black also threatens to play 8 ... Nxc3 9 bxc3 giving White doubled Pawns.

8 Qc2

White defends the Knight on c3 a second time while threatening to win the Black Knight with 9 Nxe4. I teach my students a saying to help them to remember Black's next move: "Black's next move is recommended by the two great Soviet chess Masters, Swapoff and Tradeoff." See if you can find Black's best move in Diagram 231.

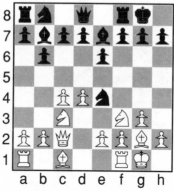

Diagram 231. *Position after 8 Qc2.*

8 ... Nxc3

It's best to swap off (or trade off) the Knight. Defending it with 8 . . . d5 allows 9 Nxe4, giving Black doubled Pawns after 9 . . . dxe4. Also, 8 . . . f5 would be met by 9 Ne5, attacking the Knight on e4 a third time with the Bishop on g2.

9 Qxc3 f5

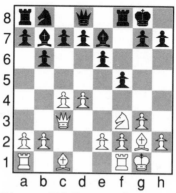

Diagram 232. *Position after 9 . . . f5.*

Black attacks the important e4 square again. This also opens up the "e8–h5" diagonal for possible future use by the Black Queen.

10 b3

White prepares to fianchetto the other Bishop on b2.

10 . . . Bf6

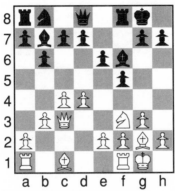

Diagram 233. Position after 10 . . . Bf6.

The Bishop pins the White "d" Pawn and directly attacks the center. After *11 Bb2* Black can play *11 . . . d6* in order to prepare to develop the Knight to d7. Part of Black's plan may involve placing the Queen on e7, supporting the advance of the "c" or "e" Pawn. Or Black can move the Queen to e8, placing it on the "e8–h5" diagonal.

Now that you've learned an opening system, it's time to learn more about the use of Pawns. As I said earlier, a Pawn can make all the difference in a chess game.

LESSON

17

💀💀💀💀💀💀💀💀💀💀💀💀💀💀

THE USE OF PAWNS

François-Andre Philidor, one of the great chess players of the eighteenth century, said, "The Pawn is the soul of chess." Pawns form the backbone of your army. Using Pawns correctly is an important skill and should be part of your long-range planning in every game you play. In this lesson we'll look at some of the weak and strong points of Pawns.

DOUBLED PAWNS

This is one of the most common weaknesses of Pawns. I mentioned earlier that doubled Pawns are two pawns of the same color on the same file. In Diagram 234 we have an example of doubled "f" Pawns.

As a general rule of thumb: Doubled Pawns are more difficult to defend and less mobile (able to move) than pawns that aren't doubled. You'll only double your Pawns by making a capture with one. Since capturing pieces is important, it's sometimes hard to avoid doubling Pawns during your game.

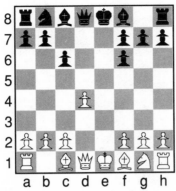

Diagram 234. The Black "f" Pawns are doubled.

There are some advantages, though, to doubling Pawns *early* in the game. First, doubling Pawns will usually open a file—and an open file can be useful for a Rook. Second, if you capture toward the center with your Pawn, this can give you a stronger center. Remember: When you make a Pawn capture early in the game you should capture *toward* the center—though there are exceptions to this general rule.

But these good points may not be as good as the bad points are bad. Doubled Pawns can't protect one another, so they make easy targets. This is especially true in the endgame.

ISOLATED PAWNS

An "isolated Pawn" is a Pawn that has no Pawns of the same color on the adjacent files (files on either side of the Pawn). In Diagram 235 the "d" Pawn is isolated.

Isolated Pawns are often weak because they can't be defended by other Pawns. If an isolated Pawn is attacked, you usually end up tying down a more important piece to defend it.

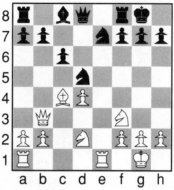

Diagram 235. White has an isolated Pawn on d4.

BACKWARD PAWNS

A "backward Pawn" is a Pawn that lags behind other Pawns of the same color. It is just as weak as an isolated Pawn, because it also can't be defended by other Pawns. In Diagram 236 the Black "a" Pawn is "backward."

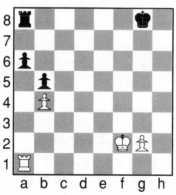

Diagram 236. Black has a backward Pawn on a6.

The Pawn in Diagram 236 isn't only backward, it's also on an open file. A backward Pawn on an open file is usually a far greater weakness.

THE PAWN CHAIN

A "Pawn chain" is a diagonal row of Pawns. Each Pawn is defended by the one behind it, except for the Pawn at the base (the bottom). In Diagram 237 the White Pawns on b2, c3, d4, and e5 are a Pawn chain.

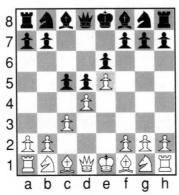

Diagram 237. White has a Pawn chain on the "a1–h8" diagonal.

The major advantage of a Pawn chain is that the Pawns are protected. It's hard for your opponent to attack a Pawn chain with anything other than Pawns. But one drawback of a Pawn chain is that all of those Pawns are on the same color squares. This means that it's hard for you to cover the squares of the opposite color.

PASSED PAWNS

A "passed Pawn" is a Pawn that has no enemy Pawns in front of it or on files next to it that can stop its advance. The "d" Pawn in Diagram 238 is a passed Pawn.

Passed Pawns are especially valuable in the endgame, when you can promote them to Queens.

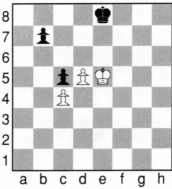

Diagram 238. White has a passed Pawn on d5.

QUEENSIDE PAWN MAJORITY

A player with a Queenside Pawn majority has more Pawns on the Queenside than the opponent does. In Diagram 239 White has a Queenside Pawn majority.

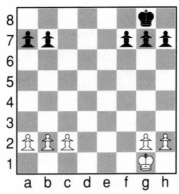

Diagram 239. White has a Queenside Pawn majority.

It's usually good to have the Queenside Pawn majority if both players have castled Kingside. On the side where a player has more Pawns there is a greater possibility of forcing a Passed pawn.

194

In the middlegame, if the players have castled Kingside, the player with the Queenside Pawn majority can advance the Queenside Pawns without exposing the King to attack. But in the endgame, if the Kings are on the *Kingside,* the Queenside Pawns can be advanced more easily because they won't run into the enemy King.

MORE ADVANCED MOTIFS

Now we can explore a few advanced strategies that can lead to capturing material or even to checkmate.

THE Qd5 DOUBLE THREAT

After putting a Bishop on c4, bringing the Queen to d5 can sometimes create a double threat! The fastest tournament game that I ever played lasted only six moves! Let's take a look at it. I played White and T. Ellis played Black in the Los Angeles Open Tournament, 1972.

1 e4 e5 2 Nf3 Nc6 3 Bc4 Nf6 4 d4 Nxe4? 5 dxe5 Bc5??

See if you can find White's move that wins a Knight in Diagram 240.

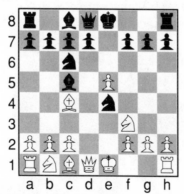

Diagram 240. Position after 5 . . . Bc5??.

White played *6 Qd5!,* attacking the undefended Knight on e4 and threatening checkmate with 7 Qxf7 + +. Black could choose between saving the Knight and being checkmated or saving the King and losing the Knight. So Black resigned. A beginner should never resign because he or she loses a Knight, but masters have resigned for far less!

I won the game in only twenty minutes. A very strong master named Larry Christiansen was playing a game on the board next to me. He went on to become an International Grandmaster, one of the highest titles in the world, *and* the United States Champion. At the end of the game he looked at me and said, "You are so lucky!" It isn't often that a game is won so quickly! Most games played between experts and masters last for hours. Indeed, I was lucky!

THE FIANCHETTO CHECKMATE THEME

The "fianchetto checkmate theme" is common against a player who fianchettos a Bishop on the Kingside and then castles on the same side. If the fianchettoed Bishop is exchanged or lost, the castled King can have serious problems. Sometimes you can set up a checkmate by using a Queen and Bishop (or even a Pawn).

In Diagram 241 White can force a checkmate in two moves. See if you can find the moves.

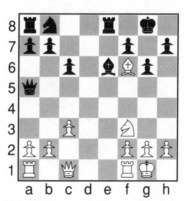

Diagram 241. White can checkmate Black in two moves.

White brings the Queen into play with **1 Qh6!**. White will be able to checkmate Black in the next move with 2 Qg7 + +.

THE CLASSIC BISHOP SACRIFICE

The "Classic Bishop Sacrifice" is used against a King that has castled on the Kingside. If you're playing White, these are some common characteristics of a position in which this sacrifice can be used:

1. The White Queen must be on either d1 or e2.
2. The White Knight must be on f3.
3. The White Bishop must be on the "b1–h7" diagonal.
4. Black must not have a Knight posted on f6.
5. The Black Pawns on the Kingside have not been moved.

If all of these conditions are met, then the Classic Bishop Sacrifice might be possible.

White will sacrifice the Bishop for the Pawn on h7 in order to expose the King to attack. The Knight on f3 will spring into action with an attack on the King, followed by the Queen on the "d1–h5" diagonal. See if you can find the winning moves in Diagram 242.

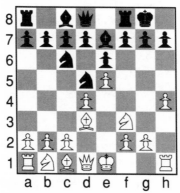

***Diagram 242.** White can use the Classic Bishop Sacrifice.*

White begins the Classic Bishop Sacrifice with *1 Bxh7+ Kxh7*. Even if Black doesn't accept the sacrifice, the Black King is still exposed to a powerful attack after 1 . . . Kh8 2 Ng5 (threatening 3 Qh5). After *1 . . . Kxh7* White continues the attack with *2 Ng5+*.

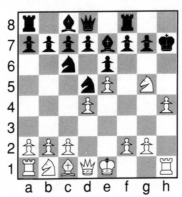

Diagram 243. Position after 2 Ng5+.

Black can choose three ways to die!

A. *2 . . . Kg6 3 h5+*: if *3 . . . Kf5*, then *4 g4++*. Or if *3 . . . Kh6*, then *4 Nxe6+* (or 4 Nxf7+), attacking the Black Queen.

B. *2 . . . Bxg5 3 hxg5+ Kg6* (if 3 . . . Kg8, then White will play 4 Qh5 f6 5 g3. Black won't be able to prevent 6 Qh8++.) followed up with *4 Qh5+ Kf5 5 Qh3+ Kg6 6 Qh7++*.

C. *2 . . . Kg8 3 Qh5 Re8 4 Qh7+ Kf8 5 Qh8++*.

BISHOP SACRIFICE ON f7 IN
THE MODERN DEFENSE

The following sacrifice exposes the King to attack because of a weak f7 square in the Modern Defense.

1 e4 g6 2 Nf3 Bg7 3 Bc4 d6 4 0–0 Nd7??

This blocks the "c8–h3" diagonal for the Black Bishop, allowing a sacrifice to expose the Black King to attack. 4 ... Nf6 is better. See if you can find White's best move in Diagram 244.

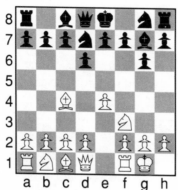

Diagram 244. *Position after 5 . . . Nd7??.*

White plays *5 Bxf7+!*, exposing the Black King to attack. If Black turns down the sacrifice with 5 . . . Kf8, then White is ahead one Pawn and has the better position. The Black King decides to take a chance and accepts the sacrifice with *5 . . . Kxf7 6 Ng5+*.

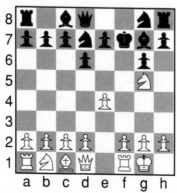

Diagram 245. *Position after 6 Ng5+.*

The Knight is attacking the King and opens up the "d1–h5" diagonal for the Queen to come into the attack. Black can move the King to one of three squares:

A. *6 . . . Ke8.* White can trap the Black Queen with *7 Ne6!*

B. *6 . . . Kf8.* White can fork the Black King and Queen with *7 Ne6+*. Not 7 Qf3+, because 7 . . . Ndf6 saves the day!

C. *6 . . . Kf6 7 Qf3+* leads to checkmate in three moves. See if you can find the moves that lead to checkmate in Diagram 246.

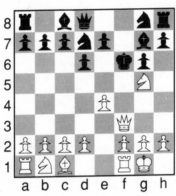

Diagram 246. Position after 7 Qf3+—White can checkmate in three moves.

Black has a choice of plan A and plan B:

A. *7 . . . Kxg5 8 d4+ Kh4 9 Qh3++.*

B. *7 . . . Ke5 8 d4+* (or: 8 Qc3+ Kf4 9 Qg3++ or 8 Qg3+ Kf6 9 Qf4++) *8 . . . Kxd4 9 Qc3++.*

KNIGHT SACRIFICE ON f7 IN
THE CARO-KANN DEFENSE

Sacrifices on f7 can happen in almost any opening. Here a sacrifice is made against the weak "f" Pawn in the Caro-Kann Defense (which I covered in Lesson Fourteen).

1 e4 c6 2 d4 d5 3 Nc3 dxe4 4 Nxe4 Nd7 5 Bc4 Ngf6 6 Ng5

This threatens 7 Bxf7 + +.

6 . . . e6 7 Qe2 Be7??

This obvious-looking developing move is a fatal mistake. Black should play 7 . . . Nb6, which can be followed by: 8 Bd3 h6 9 N5f3 c5 10 dxc5 Bxc5 11 Ne5 Nbd7 12 Ngf3.

See if you can find White's winning move in Diagram 247.

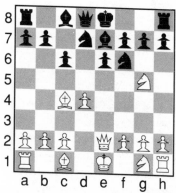

Diagram 247. Position after 7 . . . Be7??—White to move and win.

White sacrifices a Knight in order to expose the Black King to an attack with *8 Nxf7!*, forking the Black Queen and Rook. Black will be checkmated after *8 . . . Kxf7 9 Qxe6+ Kg6 10 Bd3+ Kh5 11 Qh3+ +*.

A KING AND MULTIPLE-PAWN ENDGAME

The position in Diagram 248 shows how important it is to Queen a Pawn in the endgame. White can win as a result of one key move.

The Dumb but Happy Kingdom

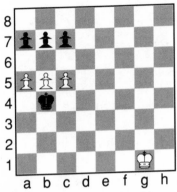

Diagram 248. White can win with one move.

I often tell my students a story that helps them to find the winning moves for White in the above position:

Once "a Pawn" a time, many "moves" ago, on a chessboard far, far away, there was a dumb but happy kingdom. The birds were always chirping, the cows always gave milk, and, best of all, the movie theaters were *always* open.

Then suddenly, the happiness was threatened. The birds stopped chirping, the cows stopped giving milk and, worst of all, the movie theaters closed! The Black King of an enemy kingdom was about to eat up the last remaining White Pawns. It looked hopeless for the Kingdom. The White King called on the wisest men in the land to find a solution.

Luckily a Knight happened to pass through the Kingdom (it was also a chess master!). After studying the position, it came up with the winning idea that would save the Kingdom. However, it needed two of the three remaining Pawns to sacrifice themselves so that the last Pawn could become a Queen. See if you can find the moves in Diagram 248 that White made to save the Kingdom.

Here are White's winning moves:
1 b6!

The Pawn immediately attacks the Black "a" and "c" Pawns, forcing Black to capture it. White couldn't have made progress with either 1 a6 or 1 c6.

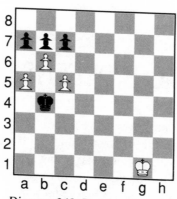

Diagram 249. *Position after 1 b6!*

Now White can capture in two ways:

A. **1 . . . axb6 2 c6!** The key move: The Pawn on c6 threatens to capture the Black Pawn on b7 and march on to become a Queen. **2 . . . bxc6 3 a6!** and the Pawn will become a Queen after **4 a7** and **5 a8=Q**.

B. **1 . . . cxb6 2 a6! bxa6 3 c6!** and the Pawn marches to c8 and becomes a Queen.

The Kingdom was saved!

But that was a *dumb* kingdom—it shouldn't have come that close to defeat. In the next lesson, I'll show you how to run a *smart* kingdom! One of the best ways to learn this is by studying history and analyzing how other players succeeded or failed.

18

▰▰▰▰▰▰▰▰▰▰▰▰▰

DAMIANO'S DEFENSE GAME

In this and the next lesson we'll look at examples of famous games from beginning to end. You'll see how to take advantage of weak opening play using sharp tactical play!

A master will be playing White in these games. See if you can find White's best moves before looking at the answers. (If you haven't been doing so, set up a chessboard so you can follow the moves.) Follow the analysis on your board and *then* check the diagram. Be sure you reset your board to the correct position.

In this game Black uses Damiano's Defense, which is rarely seen in master play today. It is very weak for Black.

Remember, a master plays White and an amateur plays Black.

1 e4 e5 2 Nf3

The moves so far are the same as those covered in Lesson Six, when we studied the Giuoco Piano.

2 ... f6?

Black tries to defend the Pawn on e5. This weakens the "h5–e8" and "a2–g8" diagonals and stops a Knight from using f6. Sometimes beginners try to defend the "e" Pawn by playing 2 ... Bd6?, but this is weak because it blocks

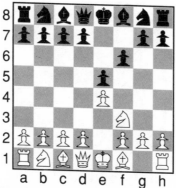

Diagram 250. *Position after 2 . . . f6.*

the "d" Pawn. Black wants to be able to move the "d" Pawn in order to open up the "c8–h3" diagonal. The natural developing move 2 . . . Nc6 is best.

3 Nxe5!

A brilliant Knight sacrifice! You should be careful not to sacrifice material without a good reason. But White has a good reason to sacrifice here: White will give up the Knight for a strong attack, which brings the Queen to the weakened "h5–e8" diagonal. White can play it safe with 3 Bc4, developing a minor piece and taking advantage of the long "a2–g8" diagonal. After 3 Nxe5! White is threatening to win more material with 4 Qh5+ g6 5 Nxg6!.

3 . . . fxe5?

Black accepts White's Knight sacrifice. This will get Black into hot water. If you are offered material and don't see why it is being given to you, look more carefully! If you *still* can't find your opponent's reason for the sacrifice, then go ahead and accept it. If you are wrong, you will have learned something new. If you are right, you will have gained an advantage in your game. In either case you come out a winner!

Diagram 251. Position after 3 . . . fxe5?.

In this case it's better for Black to turn down the sacrifice with 3 . . . Qe7, attacking the White Knight a second time. White shouldn't want to play 4 Qh5 + g6 5 Nxg6 because of 5 . . . Qxe4 +, forking the White King and Knight. However, after 3 . . . Qe7 White can get a big lead in development by playing 4 Nf3 Qxe4 + 5 Be2. The Black Queen will be a target for either 6 Nc3 or 6 0–0, with the idea of 7 Re1 putting the Rook on the open "e" file.

4 Qh5 +

The Queen forks the Black King and "e" Pawn.

4 . . . Ke7

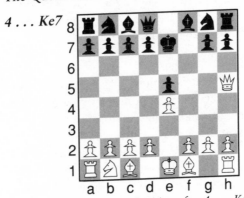

Diagram 252. Position after 4 . . . Ke7.

It's dangerous to move your King toward the center too early in the game. However, Black's only other choice loses a Rook. After 4 . . . g6 White plays 5 Qxe5 +, forking the King and Rook on h8.

5 Qxe5 +

This gets a second Pawn for the sacrificed Knight and keeps the attack on the Black King.

5 . . . Kf7

The only move that gets the King out of check.

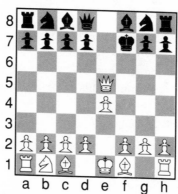

Diagram 253. Position after 5 . . . Kf7.

6 Bc4 +

White develops a new piece toward the center and continues to attack the exposed Black King.

6 . . . d5

Black decides to give up a *third* Pawn to open the "c8–h3" diagonal for the Bishop. The Bishop will cover the important f5 square.

We can see how important it is to prevent the Black Queen from going to f5: look at what happens if Black plays 6 . . . Kg6. Black loses quickly after 7 Qf5 + (White continues to attack the King and drive it toward the edge

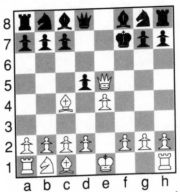

Diagram 254. Position after 6 . . . d5.

of the board) Kh6 8 d4+ (using a discovered attack by the Bishop on c1) g5 9 h4! (attacking the Pawn on g5 a *third* time and preparing to open up the Rook on the "h" file) Be7 10 hxg5+ (a double check by the Pawn and Rook). After 10 . . . Kg7 then 11 Qf7+ +.

Let's go back to Diagram 254.

7 Bxd5+

White gets a third Pawn for the sacrificed Knight and continues to attack the Black King.

7 . . . Kg6

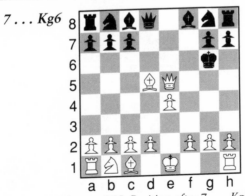

Diagram 255. Position after 7 . . . Kg6.

If 7 . . . Be6??, Black is checkmated with 8 Qxe6+ +.

208

8 h4!

White threatens to continue the attack on the Black King with 9 h5 + and attacks the important g5 square. You'll soon see why g5 is such an important square to attack.

8 . . . h5

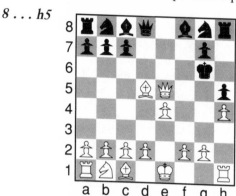

Diagram 256. Position after 8 . . . h5.

This prevents White from continuing the attack on the Black King with 9 h5 +. Black is checkmated after 8 . . . Bd6? 9 h5 + Kh6 10 d4 + g5 11 hxg6 + (en passant) Kxg6 12 Qh5 + Kf6 13 Qg5 + + or 13 Qf7 + +. However, White now has a brilliant move that forces the win of material.

9 Bxb7!

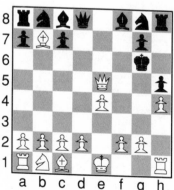

Diagram 257. Position after 9 Bxb7!.

The Black Bishop on c8 is an overworked defender. It can't defend *both* the Pawn on b7 and the important f5 square at the same time. White now wins material.

9 . . . Bd6

Black tries to counterattack by developing a new piece and threatening the White Queen. If Black captures the White Bishop with 9 . . . Bxb7, then White wins the Black Queen after 10 Qf5 + Kh6 11 d4 + g5 12 Bxg5 + . White is forking the Black King and Queen with the Bishop. The Pawn on h4 defends the Bishop on g5. This shows you how important White's eighth move was (8 h4!).

10 Qa5

White gets the Queen out of attack while keeping it actively posted.

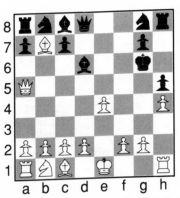

Diagram 258. *Position after 10 Qa5.*

10 . . . Nc6

The Black Knight attacks the White Queen and opens up the b8 square for the Black Rook to escape. It's better to lose a Knight than a Rook!

11 Bxc6

This wins the Knight.

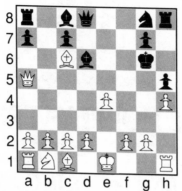

Diagram 259. Position after 11 Bxc6.

Black resigned. After 11 ... Rb8 White would have recovered the sacrificed Knight and would have been *four* Pawns ahead!

That's one way to run a smart kingdom. Let's look at it another way.

19

PAUL MORPHY VERSUS COUNT ISOUARD AND THE DUKE OF BRUNSWICK

In this very famous game Black uses Philidor's Defense. Like Damiano's Defense, this opening is rarely seen in master play today and isn't good for Black to play. The fast development of pieces in the opening gives White a powerful attack.

In this game the famous American chess champion Paul Morphy played White. As a young player Morphy was considered a genius. At the age of *twelve* he defeated the best players in New Orleans! In the late 1850s he went to Europe and won all of his matches against the world's strongest players.

This game was played in Paris, France, in 1858. The Duke of Brunswick and Count Isouard played Black against Morphy—two against one!

1 e4 e5 2 Nf3 d6

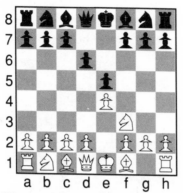

Diagram 260. *Position after 2 . . . d6.*

Black defends the Pawn on e5. However, one problem with this move is that the Bishop is blocked on the "f8–a3" diagonal. Black's position is usually cramped in Philidor's Defense.

3 d4

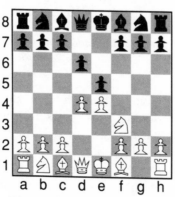

Diagram 261. *Position after 3 d4.*

White immediately attacks in the center with a Pawn and opens up the Bishop on the "c1–h6" diagonal. The Pawn on e5 is attacked more times than it is defended.

3 . . . Bg4

Black removes the White Knight as an attacker on e5 by pinning it. But the pin won't be effective very long.

4 dxe5

This will force Black to exchange the active Bishop on g4 for the White Knight.

Diagram 262. Position after 4 dxe5.

4 . . . Bxf3

Black must eliminate the White Knight on f3 before capturing the Pawn on e5. If Black tries immediately to recapture the Pawn with 4 . . . dxe5?, then White wins a Pawn *and* gets a good position after 5 Qxd8 + (forcing the Black King to move and lose the ability to castle) Kxd8 6 Nxe5. The Knight on e5 would be threatening to capture the Bishop on g4 *and* the Pawn on f7 (with a fork).

5 Qxf3

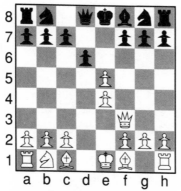

Diagram 263. Position after 5 Qxf3.

In this case it's good to bring out the Queen early in the opening. This example will help you to understand that there *are* exceptions to general rules. The Queen will be actively posted on f3 without being a target. If 5 gxf3 is played instead, White would have doubled Pawns.

5 ... dxe5

Black recaptures the Pawn.

6 Bc4

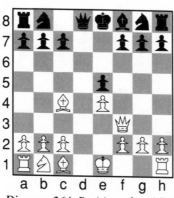

Diagram 264. Position after 6 Bc4.

215

This develops the Bishop with an attack on the Black "f" Pawn. White is threatening to checkmate Black with 7 Qxf7 + +.

6 . . . Nf6?

Black develops a Knight and blocks the White Queen from capturing the "f" Pawn. However, by not directly defending the "f" Pawn, Black allows White to use a double attack. It's better for Black to offer White an exchange of Queens with 6 . . . Qf6. White can then avoid the exchange of Queens with 7 Qb3, attacking the undefended Black "b" Pawn.

When should you trade pieces of equal value? As a general rule it is good to make equal exchanges of pieces when:

1. Your position is cramped and your pieces don't have much freedom to move.
2. When you are *ahead* in material.

With a lead in material you should usually head for the endgame by making even exchanges. With fewer pieces on the board the extra material usually makes winning easier. However, when you are ahead in material *avoid trading*

7 Qb3!

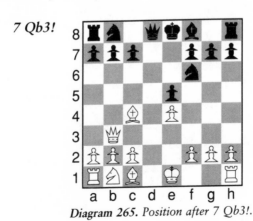

Diagram 265. Position after 7 Qb3!.

Pawns when possible. Keeping Pawns on the board usually makes it easier to win in the endgame.

White now threatens to checkmate Black with 8 Bxf7 + Kd7 9 Qe6 + +. White is also attacking the undefended Black Pawn on b7.

7 . . . Qe7

Black defends the Pawn on f7. The drawback to this move is that the Queen blocks the development of the Bishop on f8.

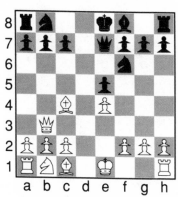

Diagram 266. Position after 7 . . . Qe7.

8 Nc3

White develops a Knight toward the center and continues to increase the attack. If White immediately grabs a Pawn with 8 Qxb7, Black can force a trade of Queens after 8 . . . Qb4 + 9 Qxb4 Bxb4 +. White would be a Pawn ahead but would have no more attack.

A very good alternative for White is 8 Bxf7 + !, planning to meet 8 . . . Qxf7? with 9 Qxb7, winning the Rook on a8. After 8 Bxf7 + Black does better to play 8 . . . Kd8 to meet 9 Qxb7 with 9 . . . Qb4 +, forcing a trade of Queens. However, in this case White would be two Pawns ahead.

8 . . . c6

This allows the Queen on e7 to defend the "b" Pawn and attack the important d5 square.

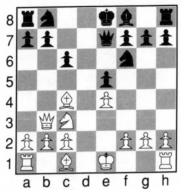
Diagram 267. *Position after 8 . . . c6.*

9 Bg5

This develops the last minor piece and pins Black's only developed minor piece—the Knight on f6.

9 . . . b5?

This weakening move allows White to play a brilliant sacrifice, which will expose the Black King to a powerful

Diagram 268. *Position after 9 . . . b5?.*

attack. Black should play 9 . . . Qc7, opening up the "f8–a3" diagonal for the Bishop on f8.

10 Nxb5!

White sacrifices the Knight for two Pawns and a strong attack.

10 . . . cxb5

Black decides to accept the sacrifice—turning it down would leave Black a Pawn down and with a bad position.

11 Bxb5 +

White captures a second Pawn and begins the attack on the Black King.

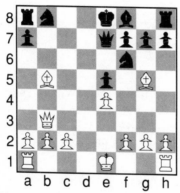

Diagram 269. Position after 11 Bxb5 +.

11 . . . Nbd7

Black blocks the check and develops a Knight. Black is in a terrible position: both Knights are pinned by Bishops, the Bishop on f8 is blocked, and the King can't castle.

12 0–0–0

White gets the King out of the center and brings the Rook onto the open "d" file. White attacks the Knight on d7 a second time and threatens to play 13 Bxd7 +.

219

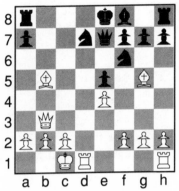

Diagram 270. Position after 12 0–0–0.

12 ... Rd8

Black brings a Rook into play in order to defend the pinned Knight on d7.

13 Rxd7!

A *second* brilliant sacrifice. White removes the Black Rook on d8 as a defender of d7 and turns it into the pinned piece. The sacrifice also clears the way for the other Rook on h1 to come to the "d" file.

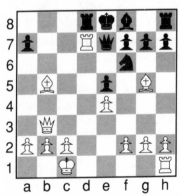

Diagram 271. Position after 13 Rxd7!.

13 . . . Rxd7

Black has no choice but to recapture material. Now the Rook on d7 is pinned to the King.

14 Rd1

White continues to pile up on the pinned piece on d7. All of White's pieces are in play.

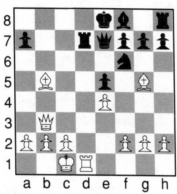

Diagram 272. Position after 14 Rd1.

14 . . . Qe6

Black opens up the "f8–a3" diagonal for the Bishop and unpins the Knight on f6. But it's too late!

15 Bxd7+

This sets up an exciting finish.

15 . . . Nxd7

Black recovers the material but allows a checkmate in two moves for White. See if you can find it!

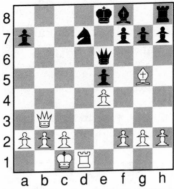

Diagram 273. Position after 15 . . . Nxd7—White can checkmate Black in two moves.

16 Qb8 + !!

Black never saw this coming. Like a bolt from the blue, White sacrifices the Queen to force a quick checkmate.

16 . . . Nxb8

The only legal move!

17 Rd8 + +

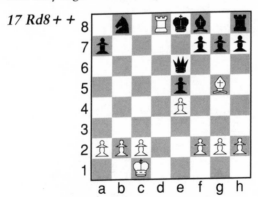

Diagram 274. Position after 17 Rd8 + +.

Black is checkmated! All of Black's extra pieces can't save the King. "All the King's horses and all the King's men can't put the Black King together again!"

CONTINUING TO IMPROVE

This is your final lesson. If you've been studying, then you're well acquainted with the basic chess strategies. But you can still improve your game in several ways.

Join a local chess club. If your school doesn't have a chess club, you can *start* one. For information on how to start a chess club in your school call or write to:

United States Chess Federation
Scholastic Director
186 Route 9W
New Windsor, NY 12550
(914) 562–8350

The United States Chess Federation (USCF) is the governing body of Chess in the United States. It is responsible for the National Chess Rating system. The USCF publishes two excellent magazines, *Chess Life* and *School Mates*. *School Mates* is written for young readers like you.

If your parents will let you, you can even spend the summer playing chess. There are several summer chess camps around the country. The camps offer chess instruction, tournaments, and other activities. For information contact:

Chess for Juniors
attn.: Robert Snyder
P.O. Box 29
Midway City, CA 92655
(714) 531–5238

If you can find a strong player or chess teacher in your area, start taking lessons. There is nothing better than having a chess coach to guide you.

Read more books! There are more books written on chess than all other games in the world *combined,* so take advantage of them! Books have been written on openings, middlegame tactics, strategy, endgames, chess history, master games, and much, much more. Collecting chess books can be a lot of fun. My personal collection has more than 1,300 chess books. Some of them were written before the Civil War!

DESCRIPTIVE NOTATION

As you read up on chess, you'll find that many older books use "descriptive" notation. This system is explained below. Descriptive notation has some drawbacks: it's more difficult to learn than algebraic notation, it takes up more space, and it requires more care in making the moves understandable.

First, the board is divided into two halves, the Queenside and the Kingside, as in Diagram 275.

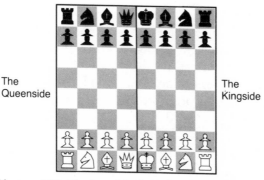

Diagram 275. The board is divided into the Kingside and Queenside.

The pieces are named starting with the Queen Rook (QR, for short) in the lower left-hand corner, as in Diagram 276.

Diagram 276.

The Pawns are named for the pieces that stand behind them. For example, the Pawn in front of White's Queen Rook is called the Queen Rook Pawn (QRP).

The files are named for the pieces that occupy them at the beginning. For example, the "a" file in algebraic notation is called the "Queen Rook file" in descriptive notation.

Each rank has two different names, one from White's side and one from Black's side. The names of the rank and the file are combined for the names of each square, as in Diagram 277.

QR1 / QR8	QN1 / QN8	QB1 / QB8	Q1 / Q8	K1 / K8	KB1 / KB8	KN1 / KN8	KR1 / KR8
QR2 / QR7	QN2 / QN7	QB2 / QB7	Q2 / Q7	K2 / K7	KB2 / KB7	KN2 / KN7	KR2 / KR7
QR3 / QR6	QN3 / QN6	QB3 / QB6	Q3 / Q6	K3 / K6	KB3 / KB6	KN3 / KN6	KR3 / KR6
QR4 / QR5	QN4 / QN5	QB4 / QB5	Q4 / Q5	K4 / K5	KB4 / KB5	KN4 / KN5	KR4 / KR5
QR5 / QR4	QN5 / QN4	QB5 / QB4	Q5 / Q4	K5 / K4	KB5 / KB4	KN5 / KN4	KR5 / KR4
QR6 / QR3	QN6 / QN3	QB6 / QB3	Q6 / Q3	K6 / K3	KB6 / KB3	KN6 / KN3	KR6 / KR3
QR7 / QR2	QN7 / QN2	QB7 / QB2	Q7 / Q2	K7 / K2	KB7 / KB2	KN7 / KN2	KR7 / KR2
QR8 / QR1	QN8 / QN1	QB8 / QB1	Q8 / Q1	K8 / K1	KB8 / KB1	KN8 / KN1	KR8 / KR1

Diagram 277.

Each square on the board has two different names, one for White and one for Black. The bottom name in each square (Diagram 277) is from White's point of view. The top name is from Black's point of view.

Most of the symbols used in descriptive notation are the same as those used in algebraic notation. The one major difference is that descriptive notation has the symbol "–" which means "to." You write it between the *name of the piece* that is moving and the *name of the square* that the piece is moving to. So P–K4 means "Pawn to King Four."

226

The following is an example of the same moves given in descriptive and algebraic notations:

Descriptive		Algebraic	
1 P–K4	P–K4	1 e4	e5
2 N–KB3	N–QB3	2 Nf3	Nc6
3 B–N5	P–QR3	3 Bb5	a6
4 BxN	QPxB	4 Bxc6	dxc6
5 0–0	B–KN5	5 0–0	Bg4

You'll note on White's second move that only one Knight could move to KB3, so N–KB3 is written instead of KN–KB3. Also, on White's third move only one Bishop could move to N5. Therefore, B–N5 was written instead of B–QN5. Shortcuts are used whenever possible.

If you've come this far, you're well on your way. Chess is an ancient game, and you can be sure that people will play it thousands of years from now. But more important, it's fun and it's fascinating. Who knows, maybe if you keep playing *you'll* become a grandmaster! It is a game of skill, to be sure, but good luck!

INDEX

˙˙˙˙˙˙˙˙˙˙˙˙˙˙˙˙˙˙

ABOUT THE AUTHOR

Robert M. Snyder is a highly regarded chess educator and well-known personality in scholastic chess circles. He has introduced chess to thousands of children through school presentations and his "Chess for Juniors" television show. His students include first-place winners at both the National Elementary and Junior High School Championships.

At the age of twelve, Mr. Snyder learned how to play chess. By the time he was eighteen, he earned the title of National Chess Master. In 1973 he became Champion of the Western United States. Mr. Snyder represented the United States on the Correspondence Olympic Team and earned an International rating of 2405.

In 1983 he founded the "Chess for Juniors" club in Garden Grove, California, which is now the largest and most active chess club for youth in the nation. He has written articles for *Chess Life* and *School Mates* magazines and is the author of *The Snyder Sicilian*.

Available from your local bookseller or

ORDER TOLL–FREE
1-800-733-3000

When ordering, please mention the following code: 005•07•CHJR

OR SEND ORDERS TO:

RANDOM HOUSE, INC.
400 Hahn Road
Westminster, MD 21157
Attn.: Order Processing

Postage & Handling Rates

First Book $2.00
Each Additional Book...$0.50

Total from other side:

Number of books:_____ Total price: $_____

☐ Check or money order enclosed $ _____ (include postage and handling)

☐ Please charge $_____to my: ☐ MASTERCARD   ☐ VISA

Account No._____ Expiration Date_____
Signature _____

Name (please print) _____

Address_____ Apt. # _____

City_____ State_____ Zip _____

Classic Titles from the McKay Chess Library

☐ 679-14108-1	**ART OF DEFENSE IN CHESS,** Andrew Soltis	$ 7.95
☐ 679-14101-4	**ART OF POSITIONAL PLAY,** Samuel Reshevsky	$ 9.95
☐ 679-14000-X	**ART OF SACRIFICE IN CHESS,** Rudolf Spielmann	$ 8.95
☐ 679-14002-6	**BASIC CHESS ENDINGS,** Reuben Fine	$14.95
☐ 679-14044-1	**CAPABLANCA'S 100 BEST GAMES OF CHESS,** H. Golombek	$ 8.95
☐ 679-14151-0	**CATALOG OF CHESS MISTAKES,** Andrew Soltis	$ 6.95
☐ 8129-1867-3	**CHESS FOR JUNIORS,** Robert Snyder	$13.00
☐ 679-14004-2	**CHESS FUNDAMENTALS,** J. R. Capablanca	$ 8.95
☐ 679-14005-0	**CHESS STRATEGY & TACTICS**, Fred Reinfeld	$ 6.95
☐ 679-14045-X	**DEVELOPMENT OF CHESS STYLE,** Dr. M. Euwe	$ 7.95
☐ 679-14109-X	**HOW TO PLAY GOOD OPENING MOVES,** Edmar Mednis	$ 6.95
☐ 679-14015-8	**HOW TO WIN IN CHESS ENDINGS,** I. A. Horowitz	$ 7.95
☐ 8129-1756-1	**IDEAS BEHIND THE CHESS OPENINGS**, Reuben Fine	$ 8.95
☐ 679-14325-4	**JUDGEMENT AND PLANNING IN CHESS,** Dr. M. Euwe	$ 6.95
☐ 8129-1923-8	**KARPOV-KASPAROV,** Don Maddox et al.	$15.00
☐ 679-14107-3	**KING POWER IN CHESS,** Edmar Mednis	$ 8.95
☐ 679-14403-X	**MAXIMS OF CHESS,** John W. Collins	$10.95
☐ 679-14021-2	**MIDDLE GAMES IN CHESS,** Reuben Fine	$10.95
☐ 8129-1785-5	**MODERN CHESS OPENINGS: New 13th Edition,** Walter Korn	$18.95
☐ 679-14103-0	**MODERN CHESS SACRIFICE,** Leonid Shamkovich	$10.95
☐ 679-14022-0	**MODERN CHESS STRATEGY,** Edward Lasker	$ 7.95
☐ 8129-1884-3	**NEW YORK TIMES CHESS BOOK OF GREAT CHESS VICTORIES AND DEFEATS,** Robert Byrne	$ 8.95
☐ 679-14154-5	**OFFICIAL RULES OF CHESS,** United States Chess Federation	$ 7.95
☐ 679-14475-7	**PAWN STRUCTURE CHESS**, Andrew Soltis	$ 8.95
☐ 679-14037-9	**WINNING CHESS TRAPS,** Irving Chernev	$ 8.95
☐ 8129-1866-5	**WINNING WITH CHESS PSYCHOLOGY,** Benko & Hochberg	$13.00

AVAILABLE IN BETTER BOOKSTORES OR SEE REVERSE SIDE
FOR ORDERING INSTRUCTIONS